INDIA
COLORING BOOK
FOR ADULTS

AN ADULT COLORING BOOK OF INDIAN INSPIRED DESIGNS INCLUDING HENNA, PAISLEY, MANDALAS AND MORE

ADULT COLORING WORLD

ISBN-13: 978-1519694058

ISBN-10: 1519694059

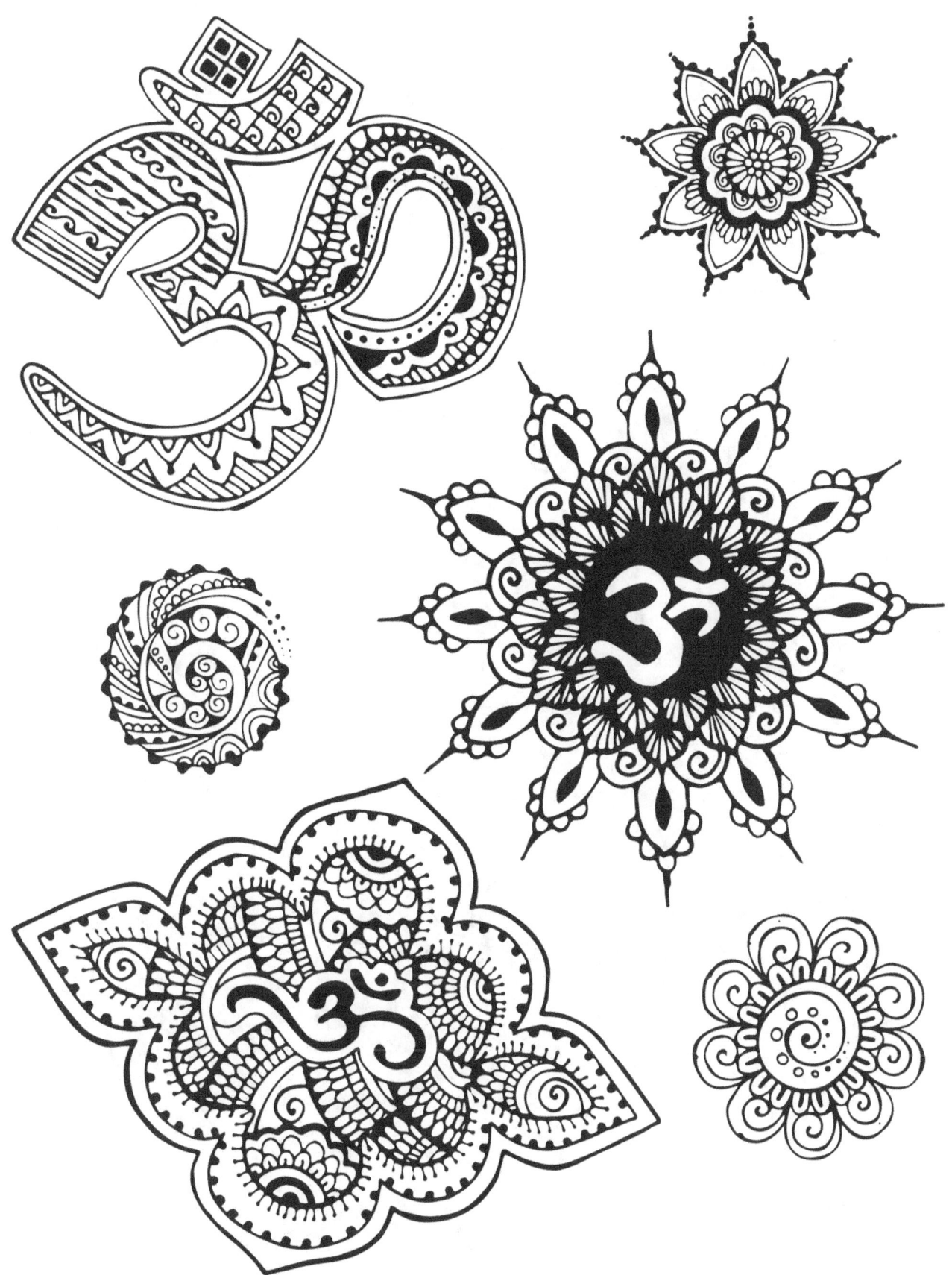

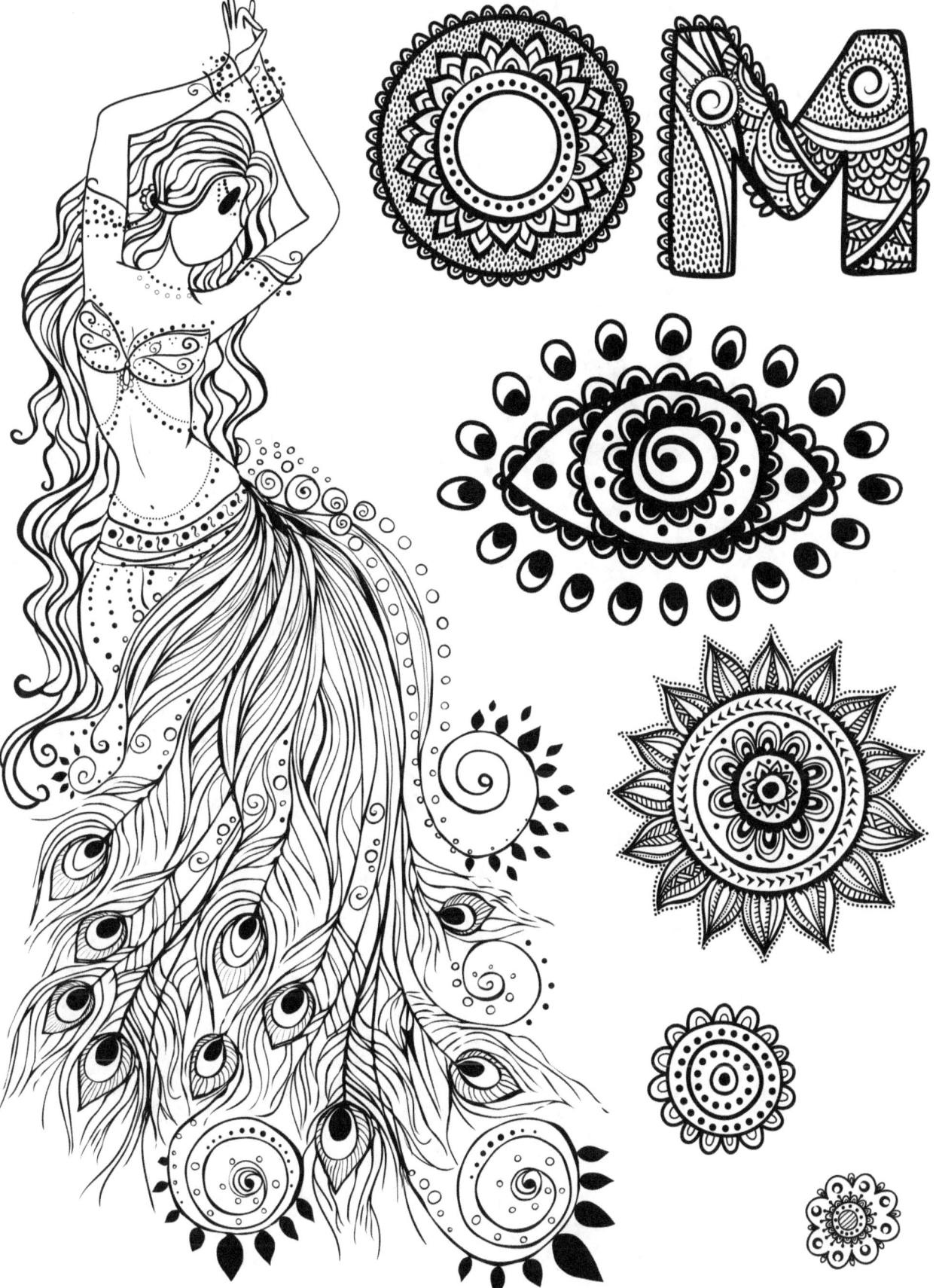

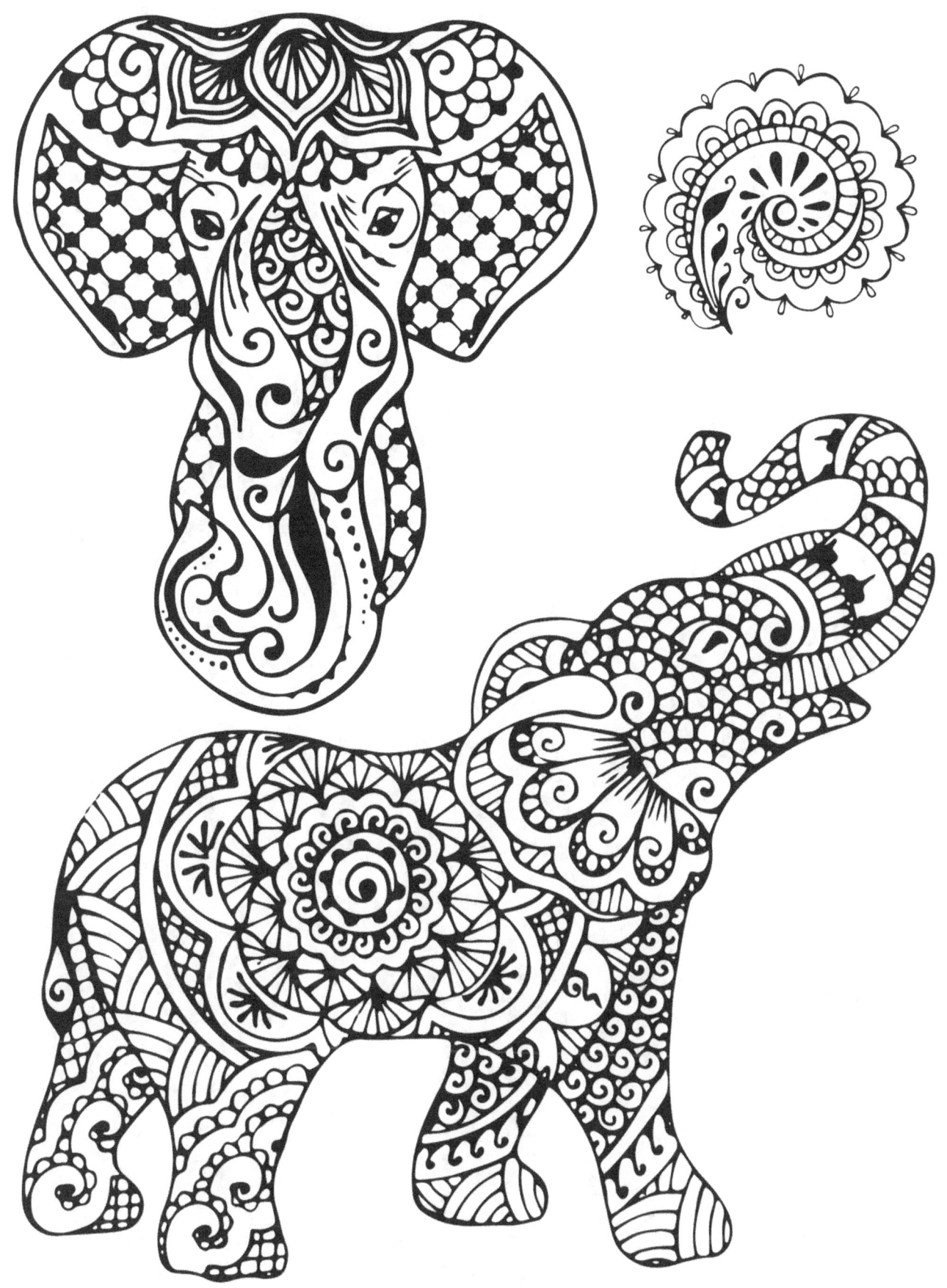

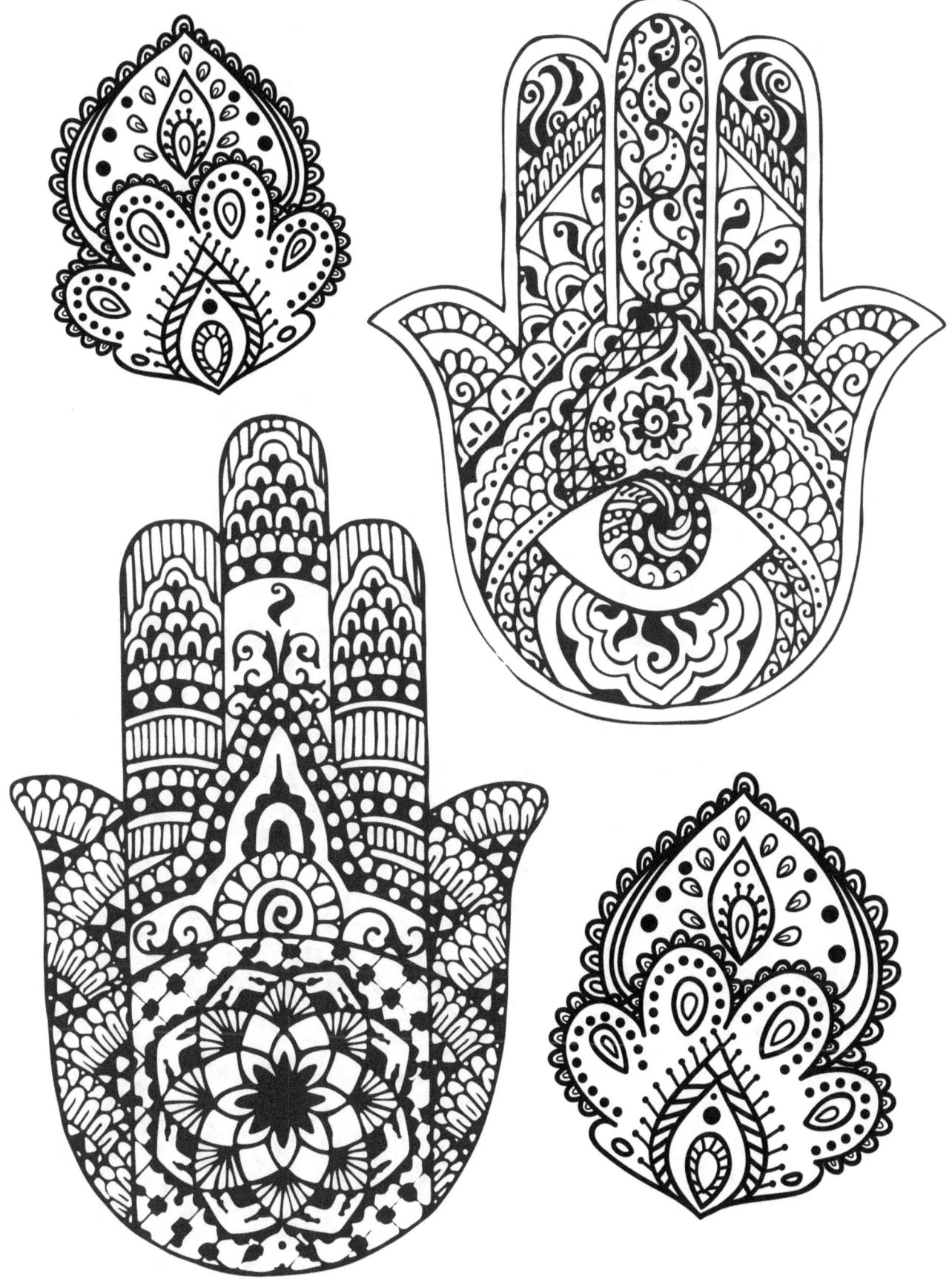

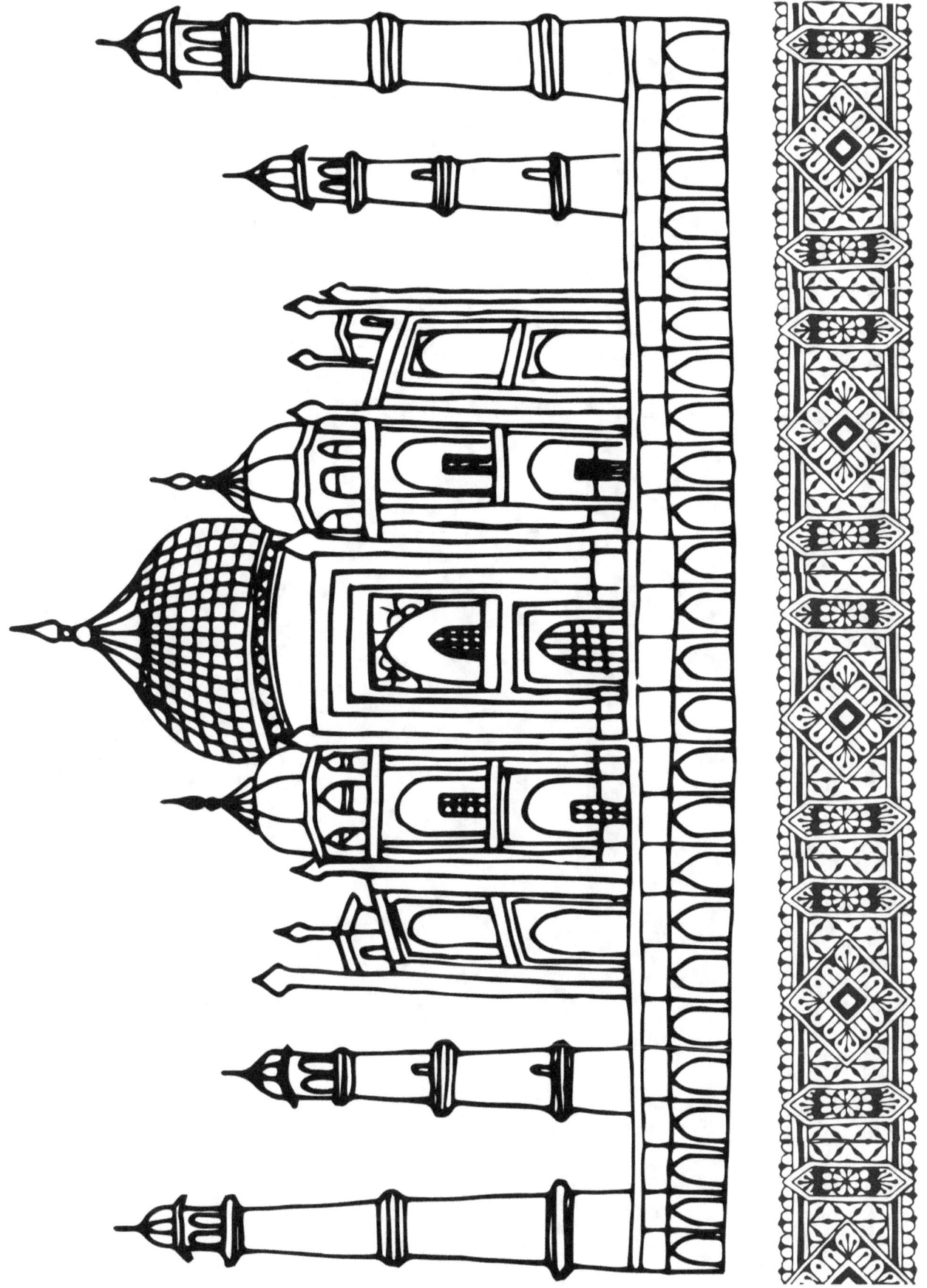

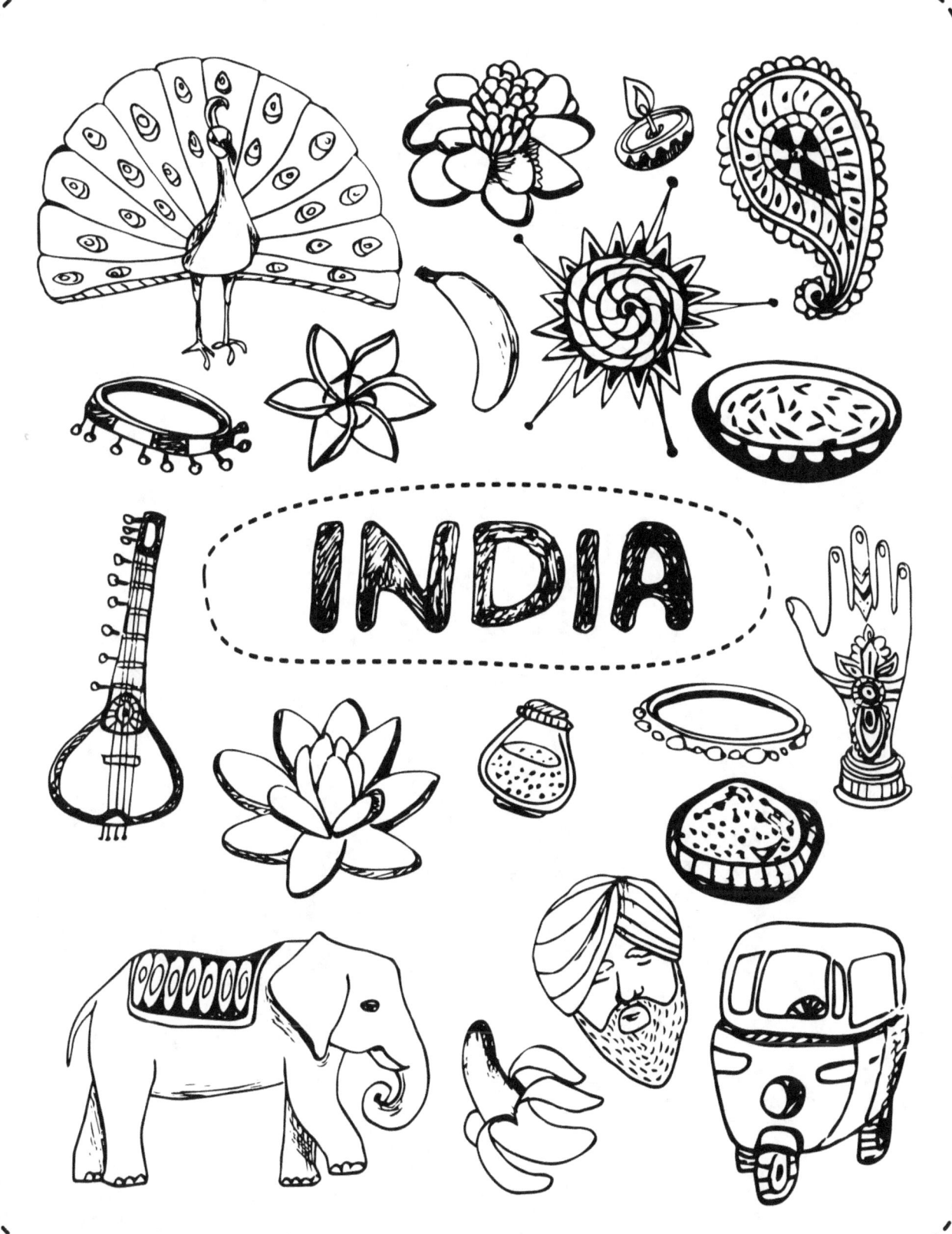

INDIA

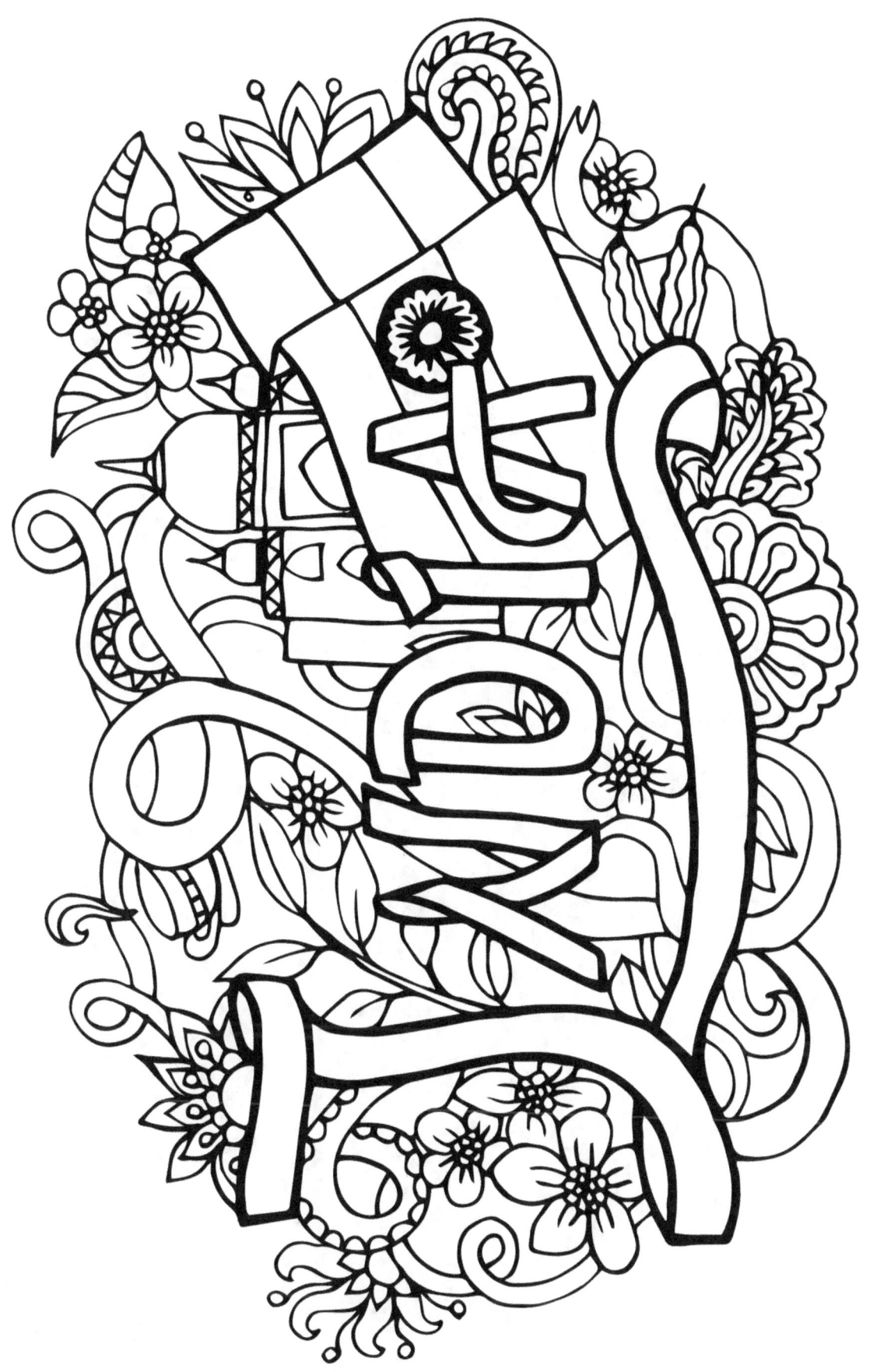

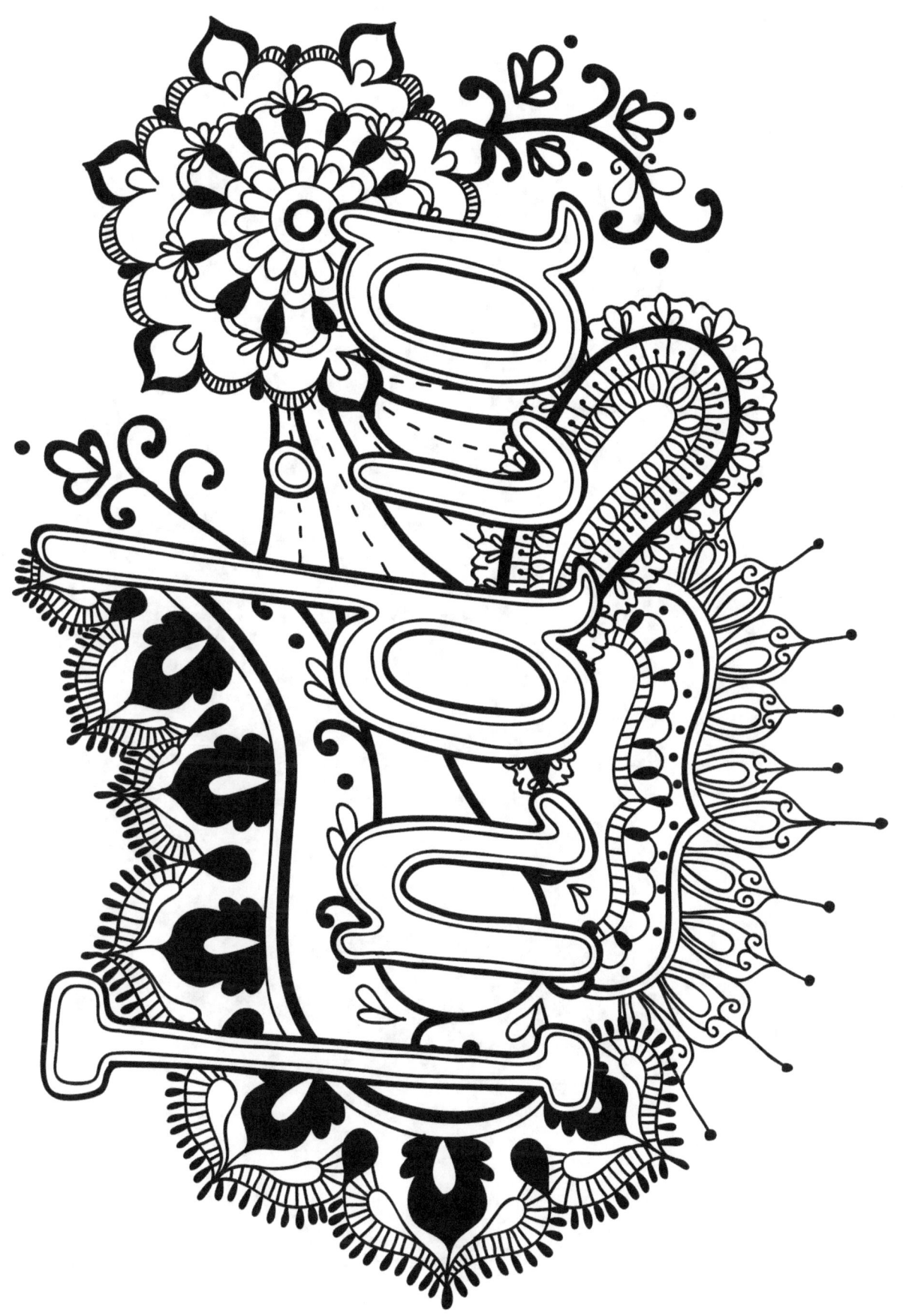

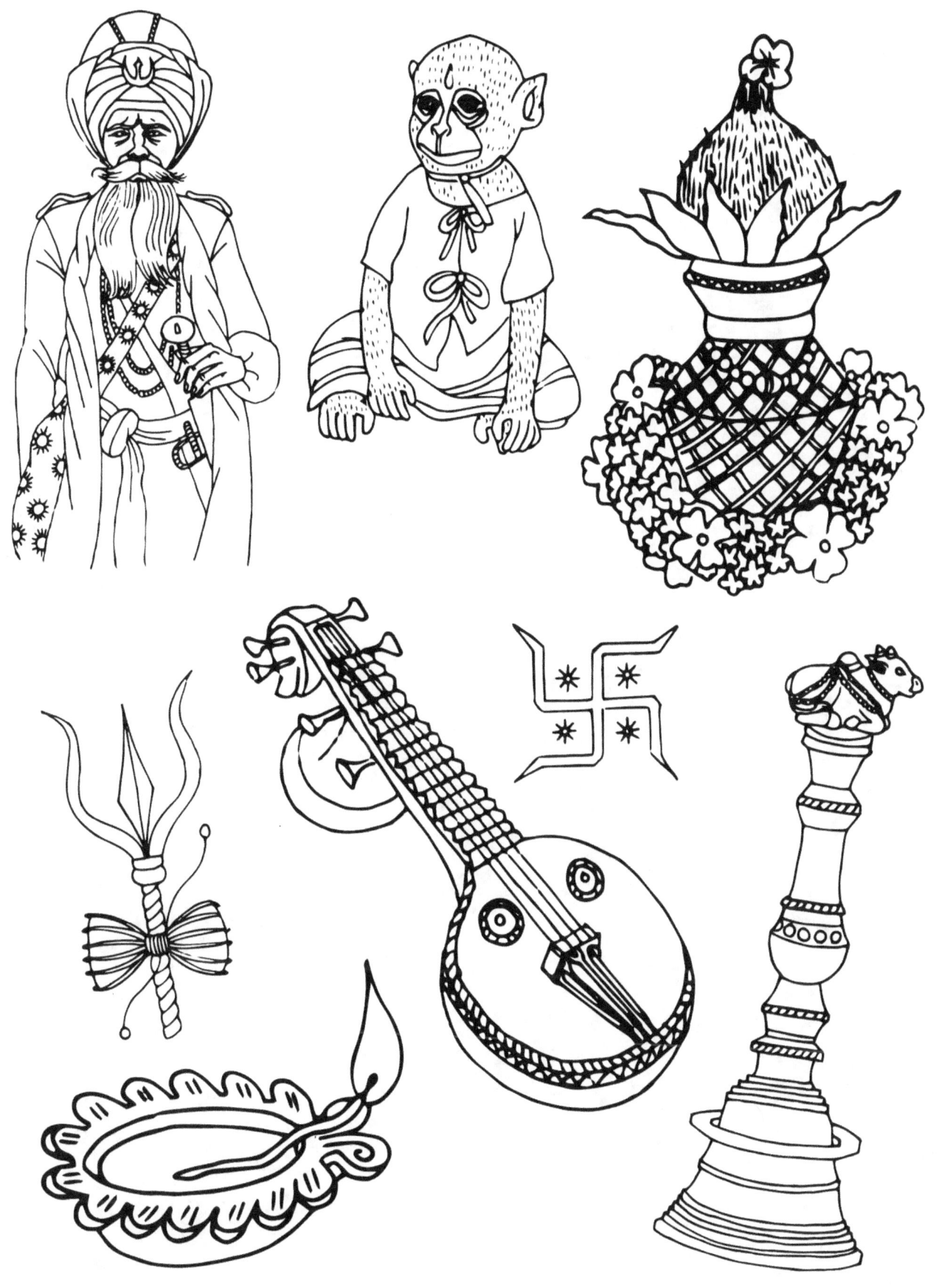

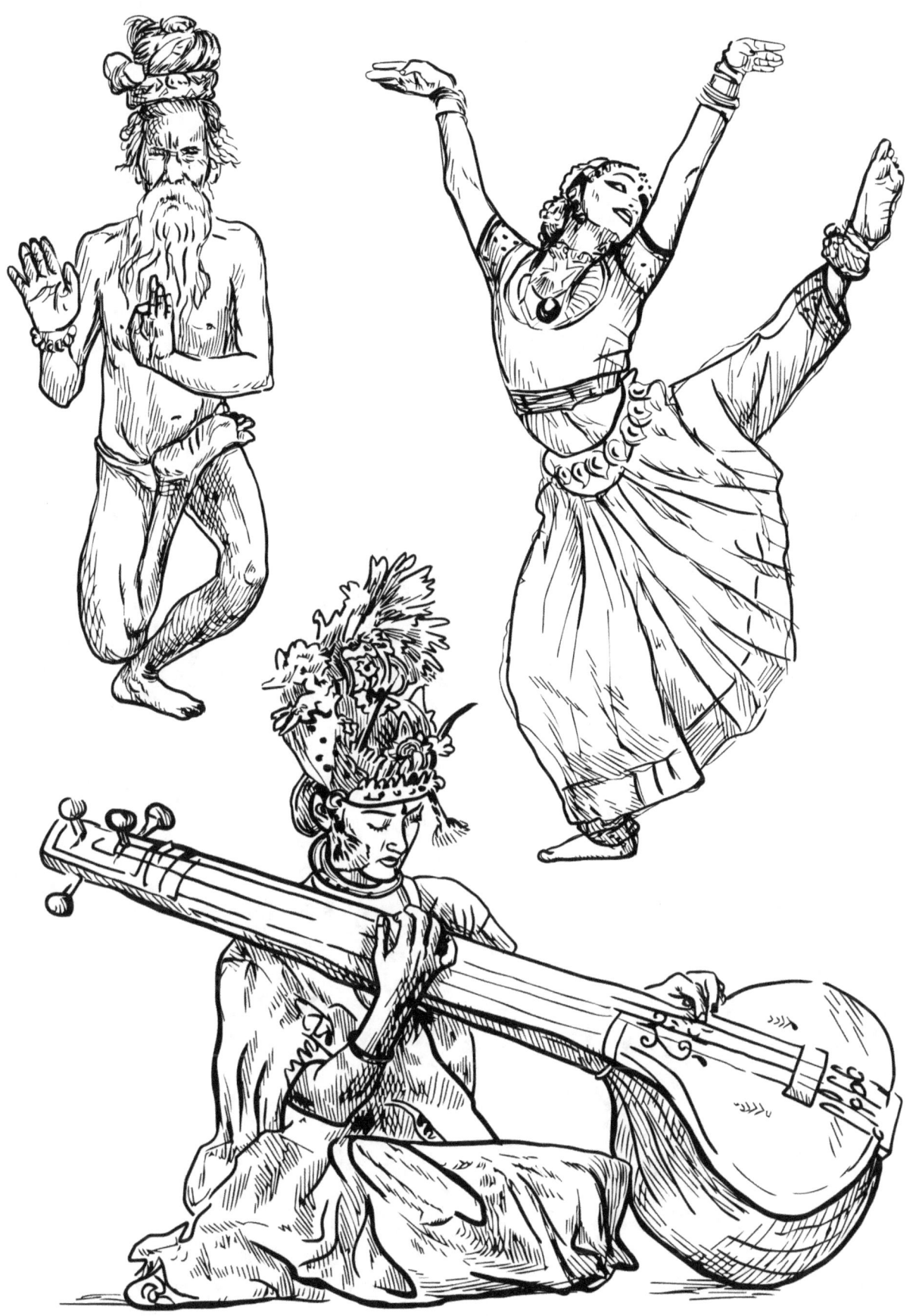

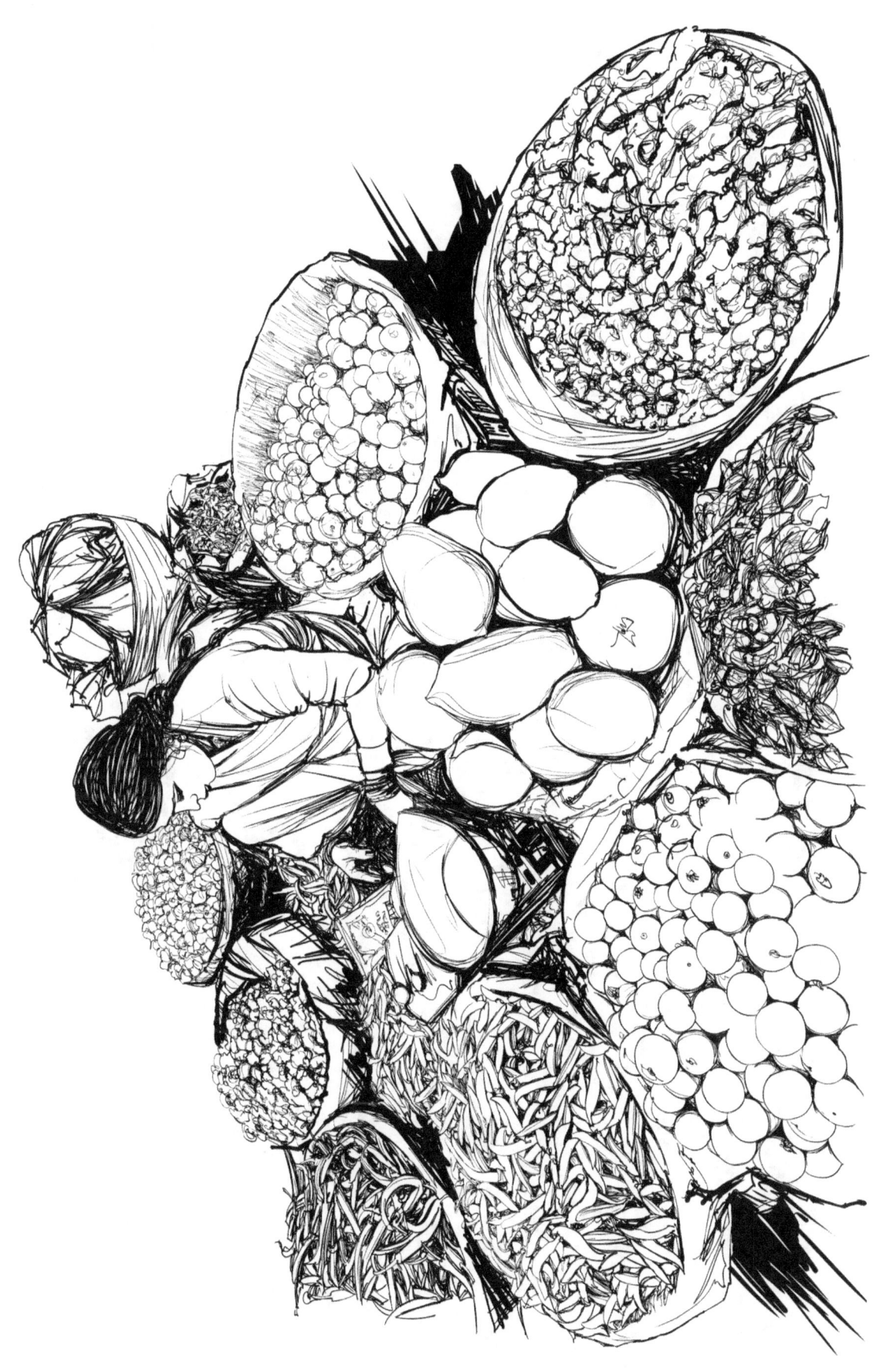

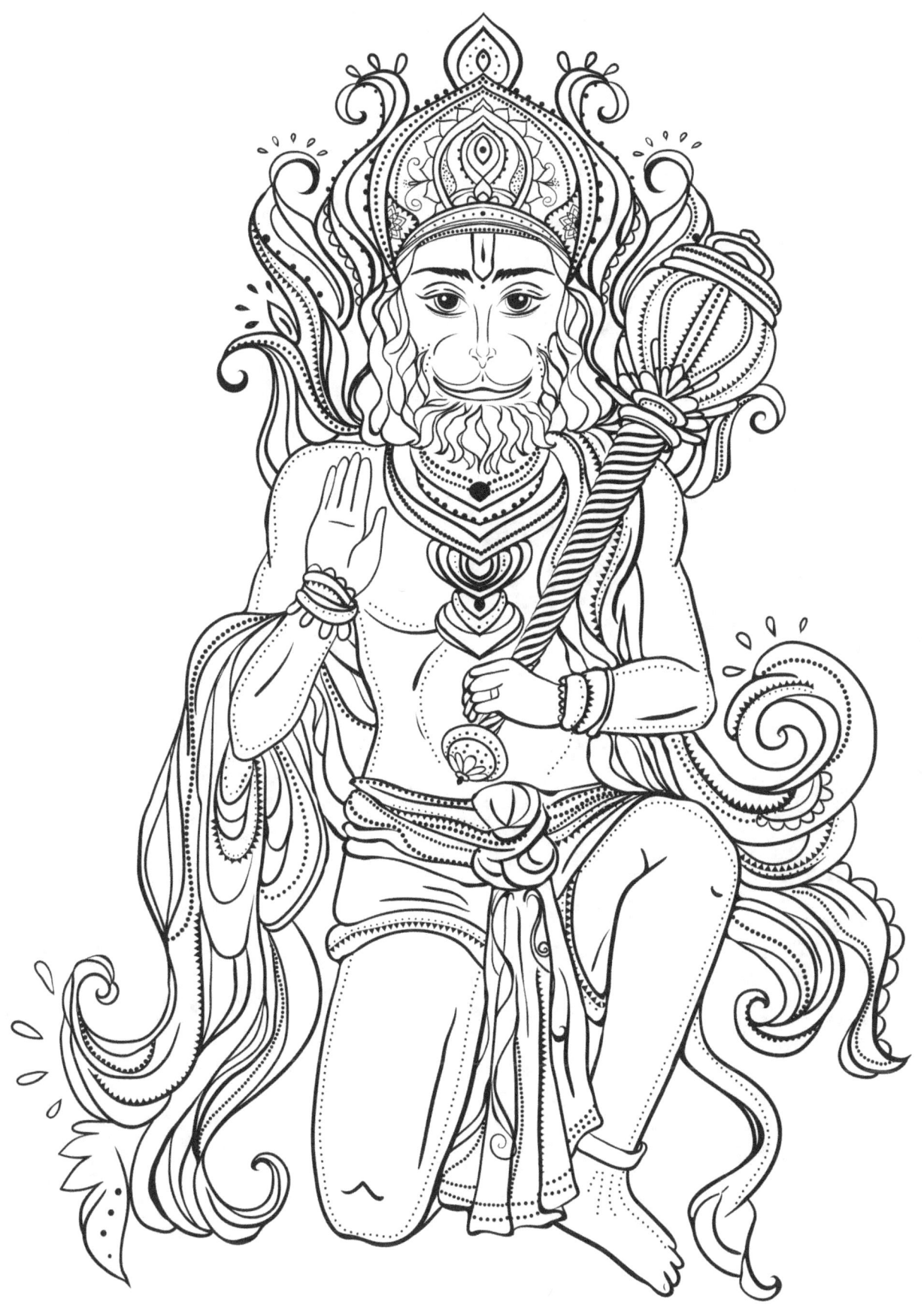

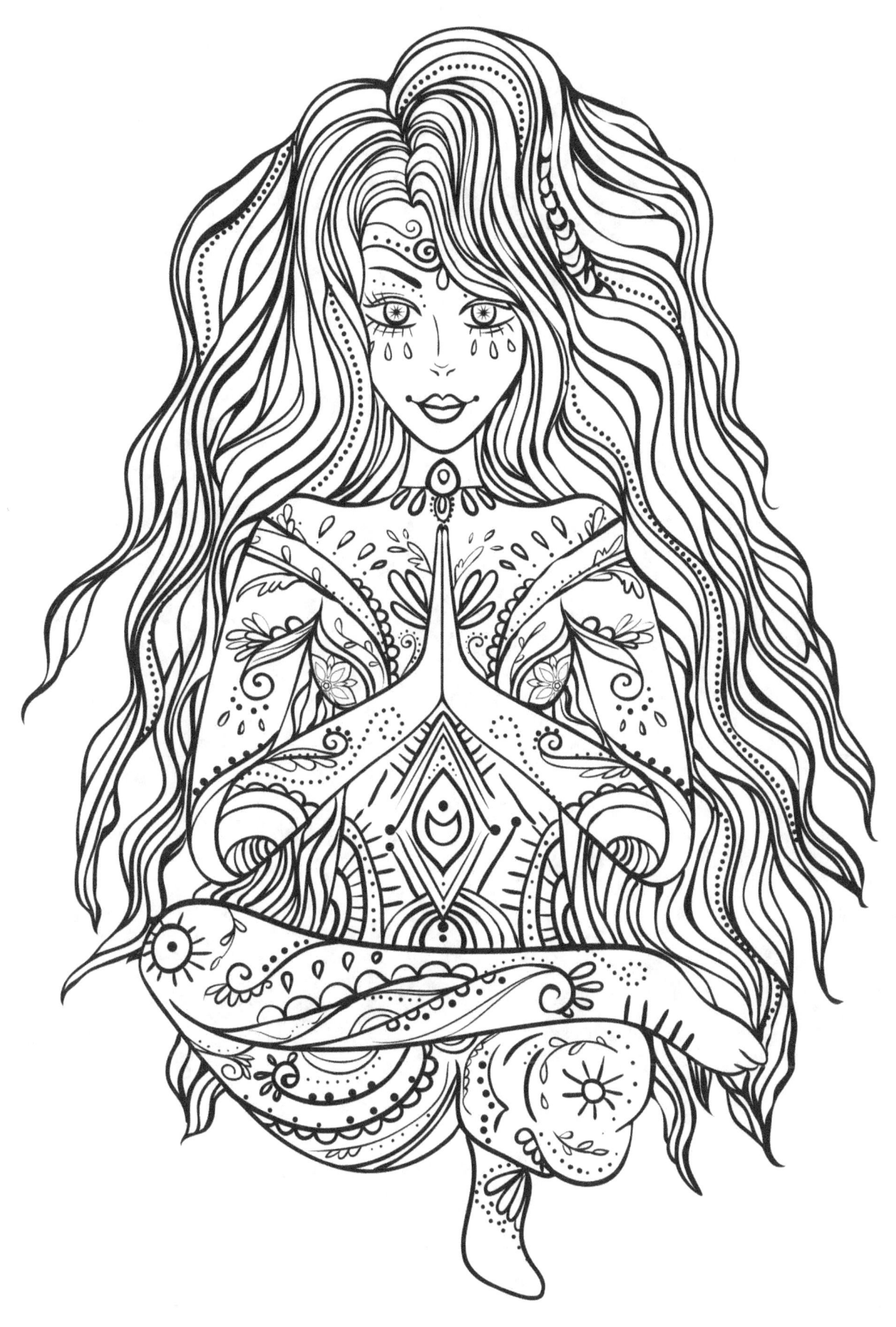

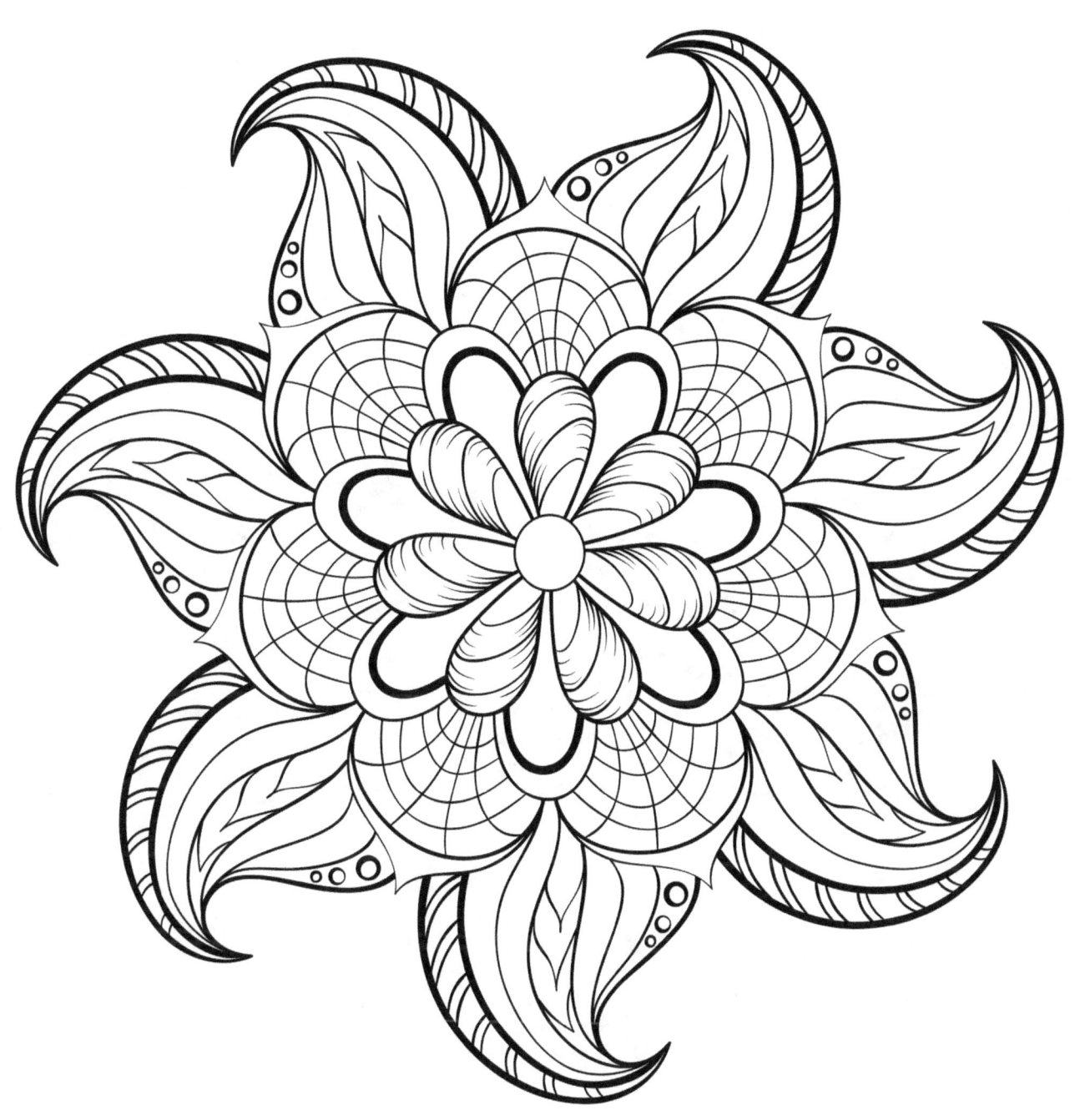

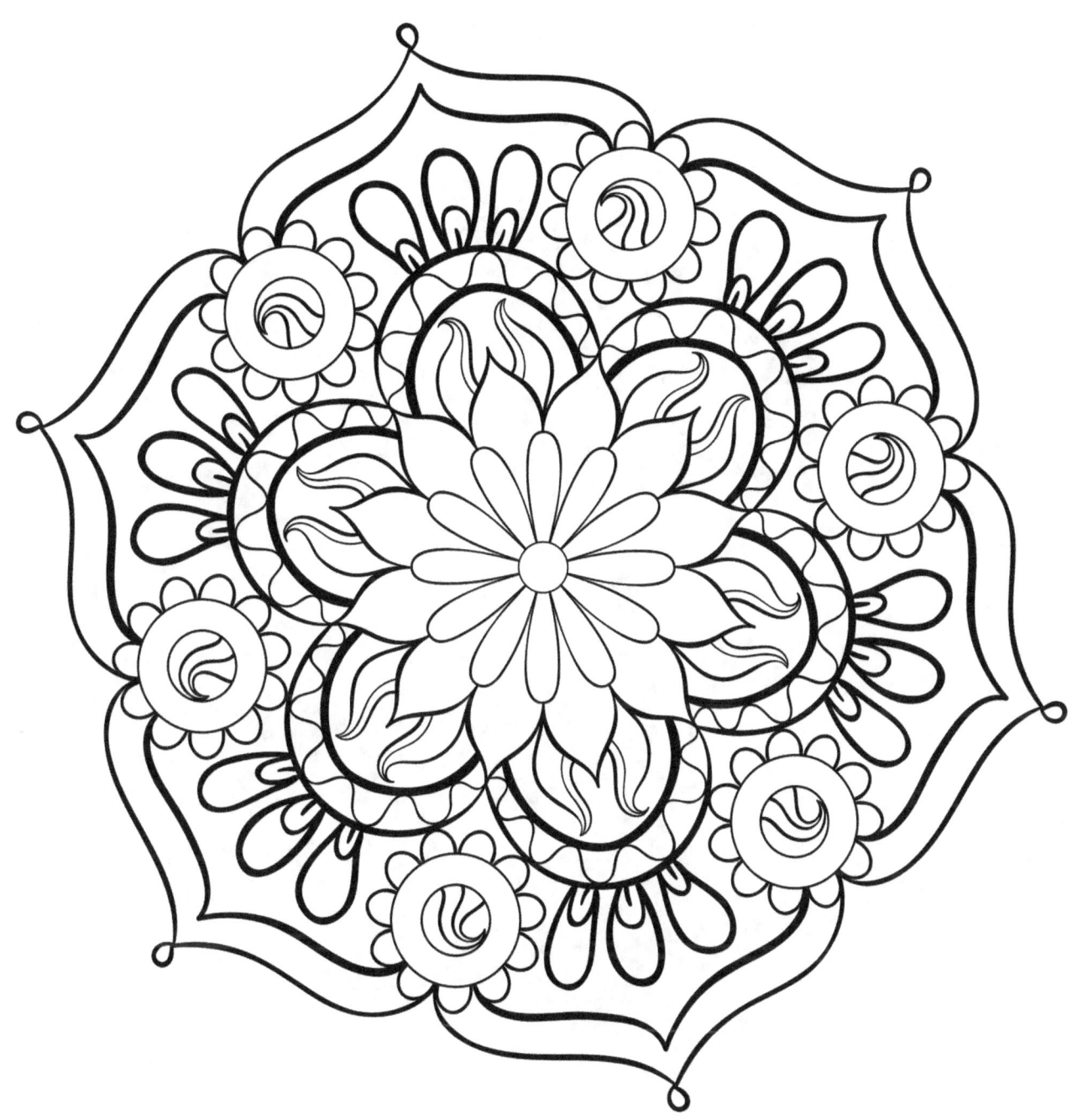

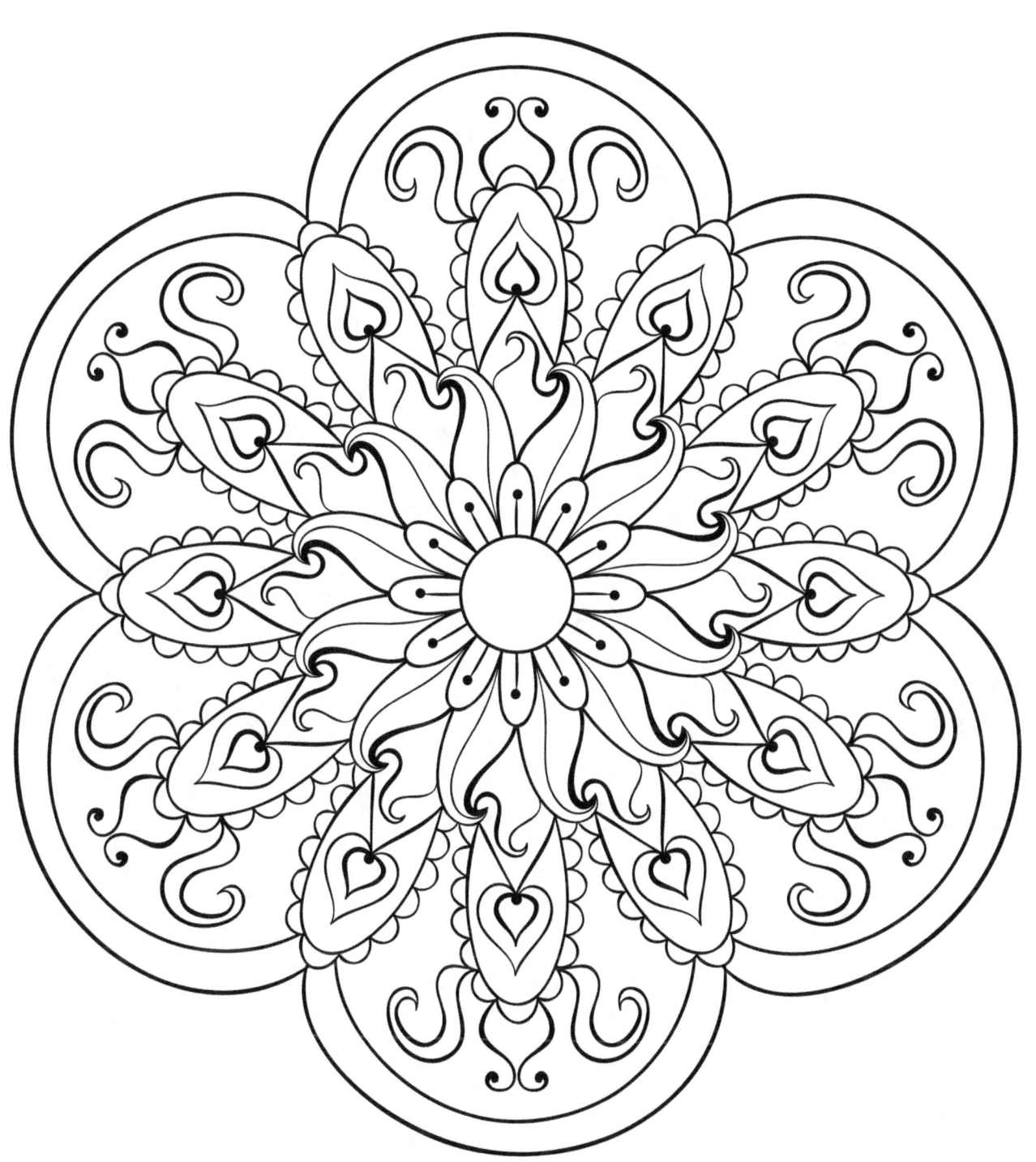

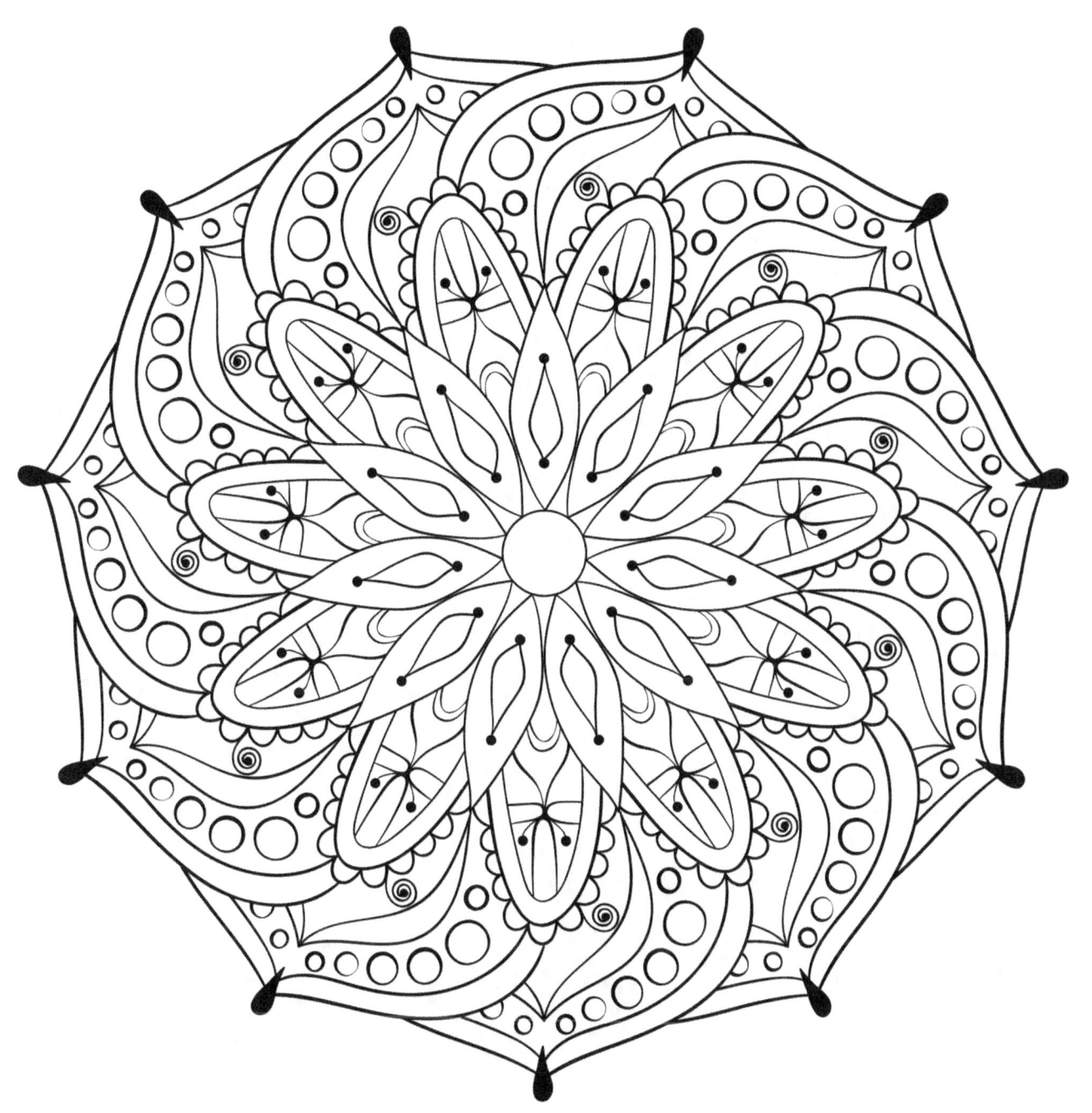

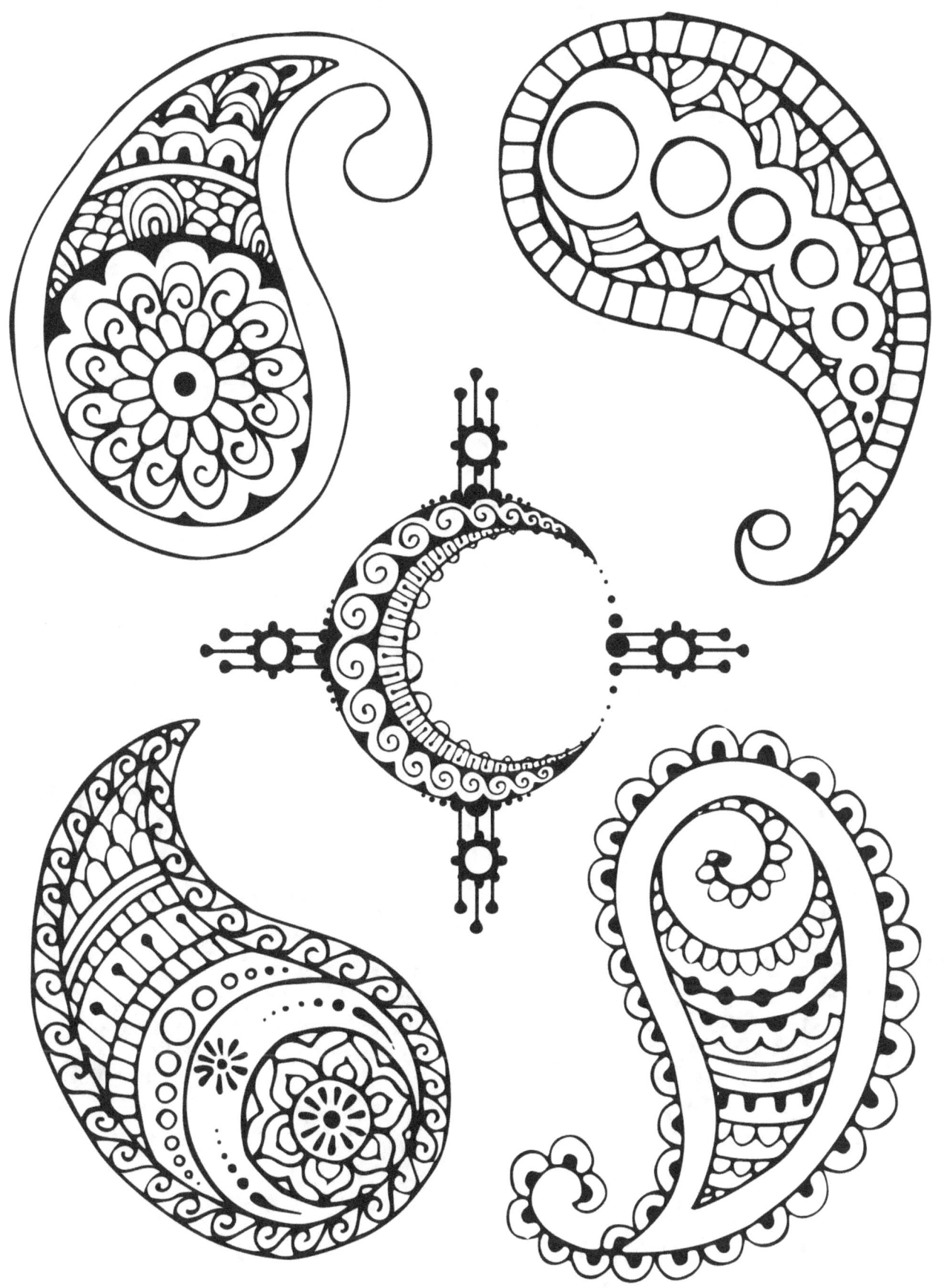

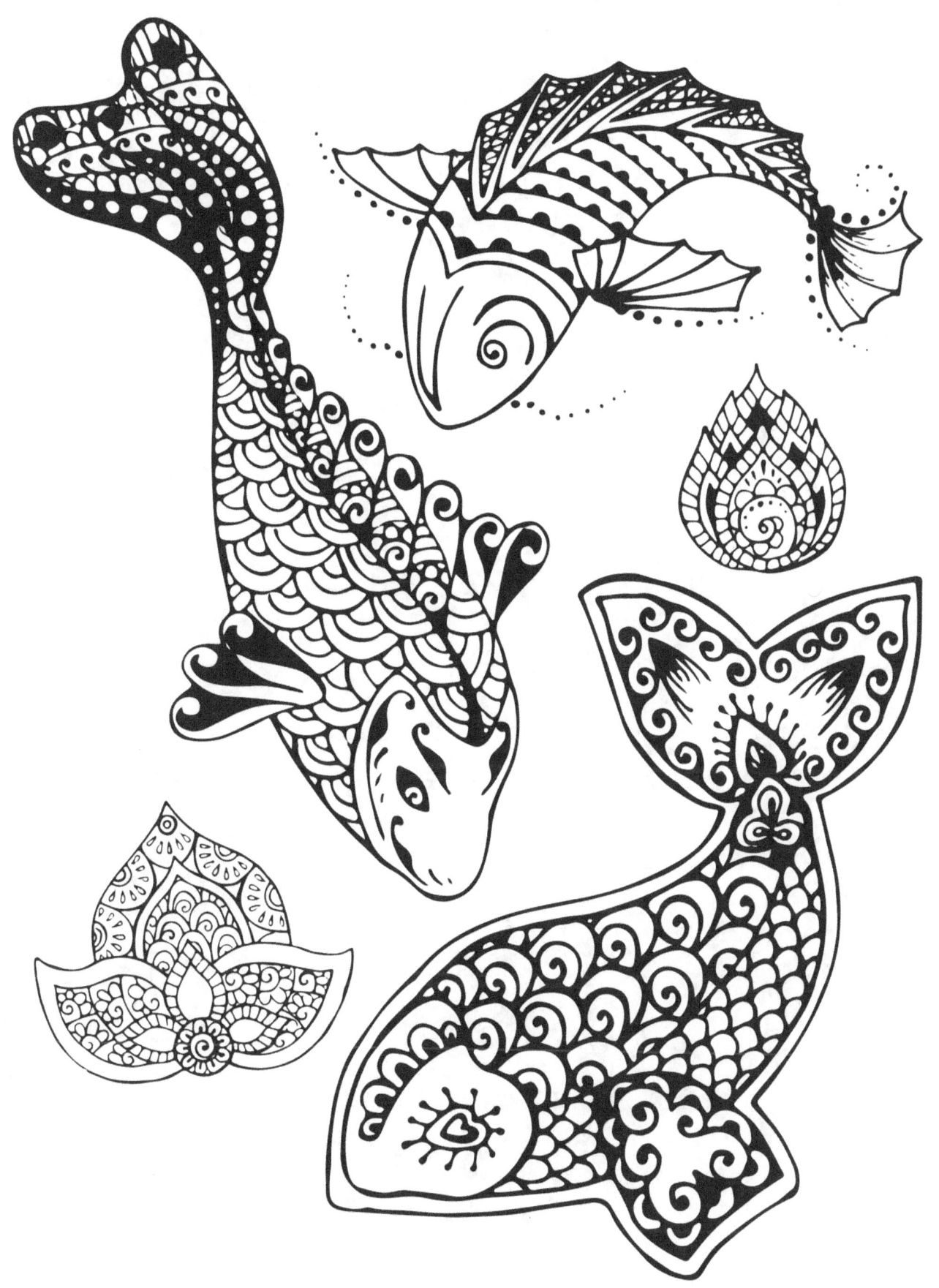

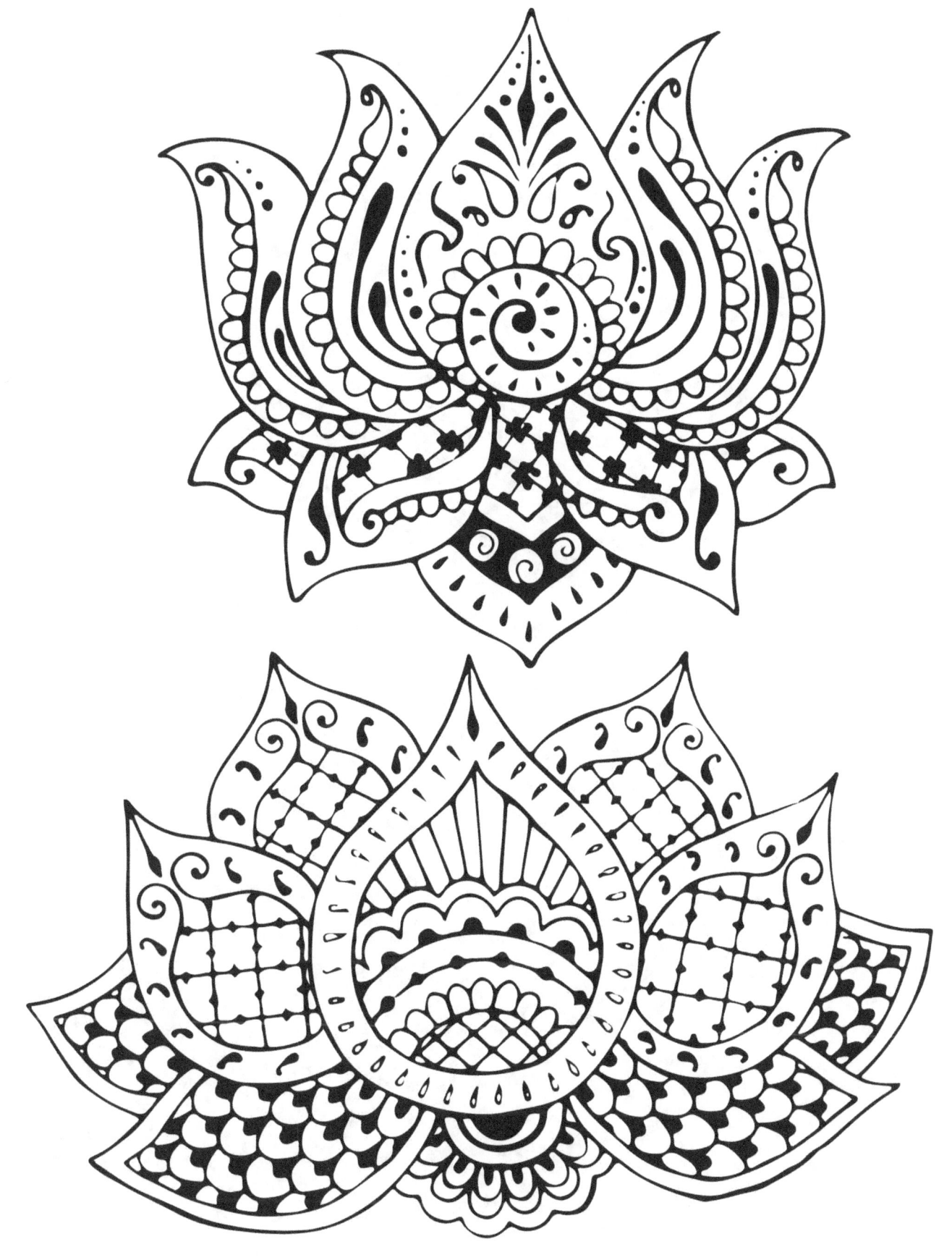

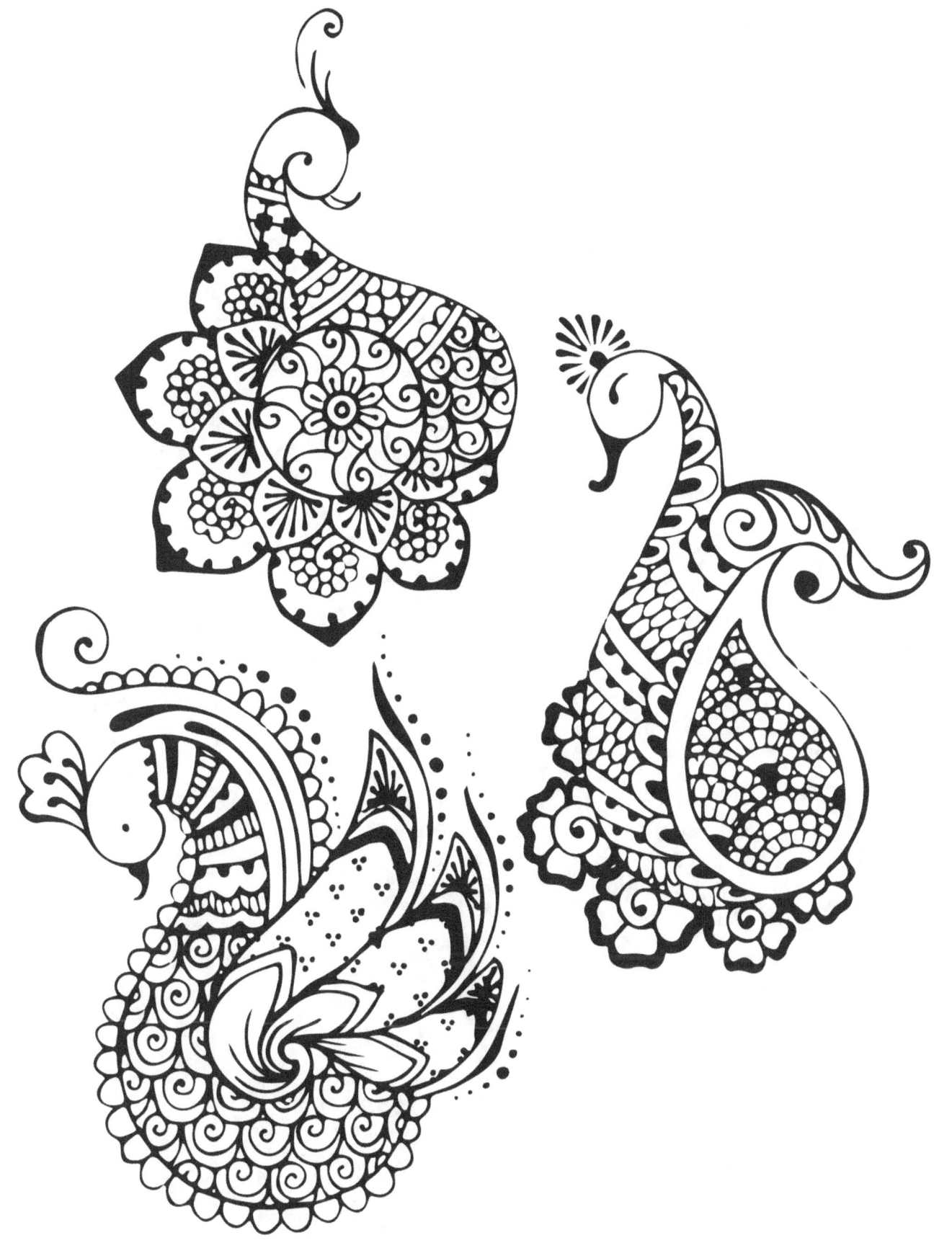

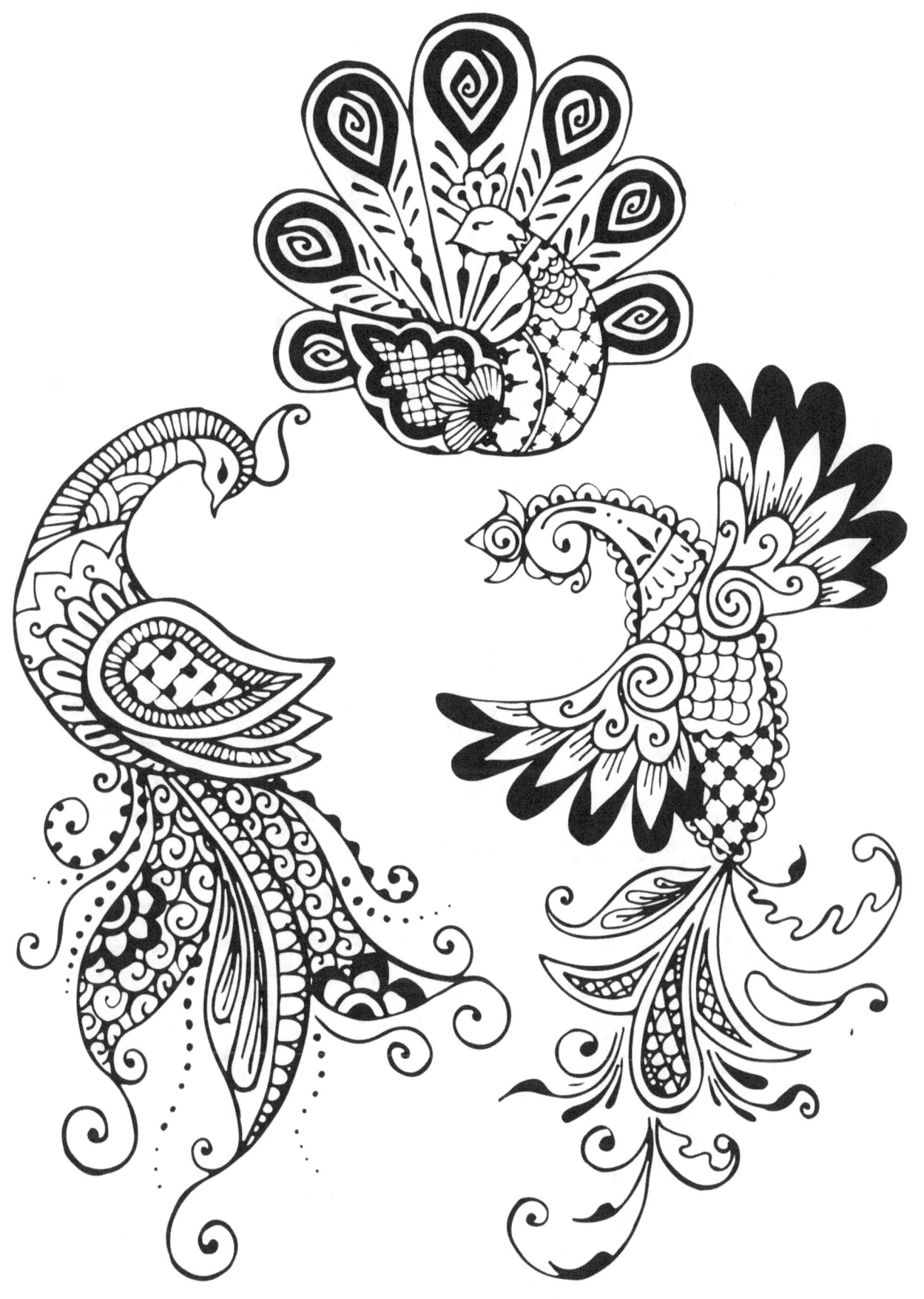

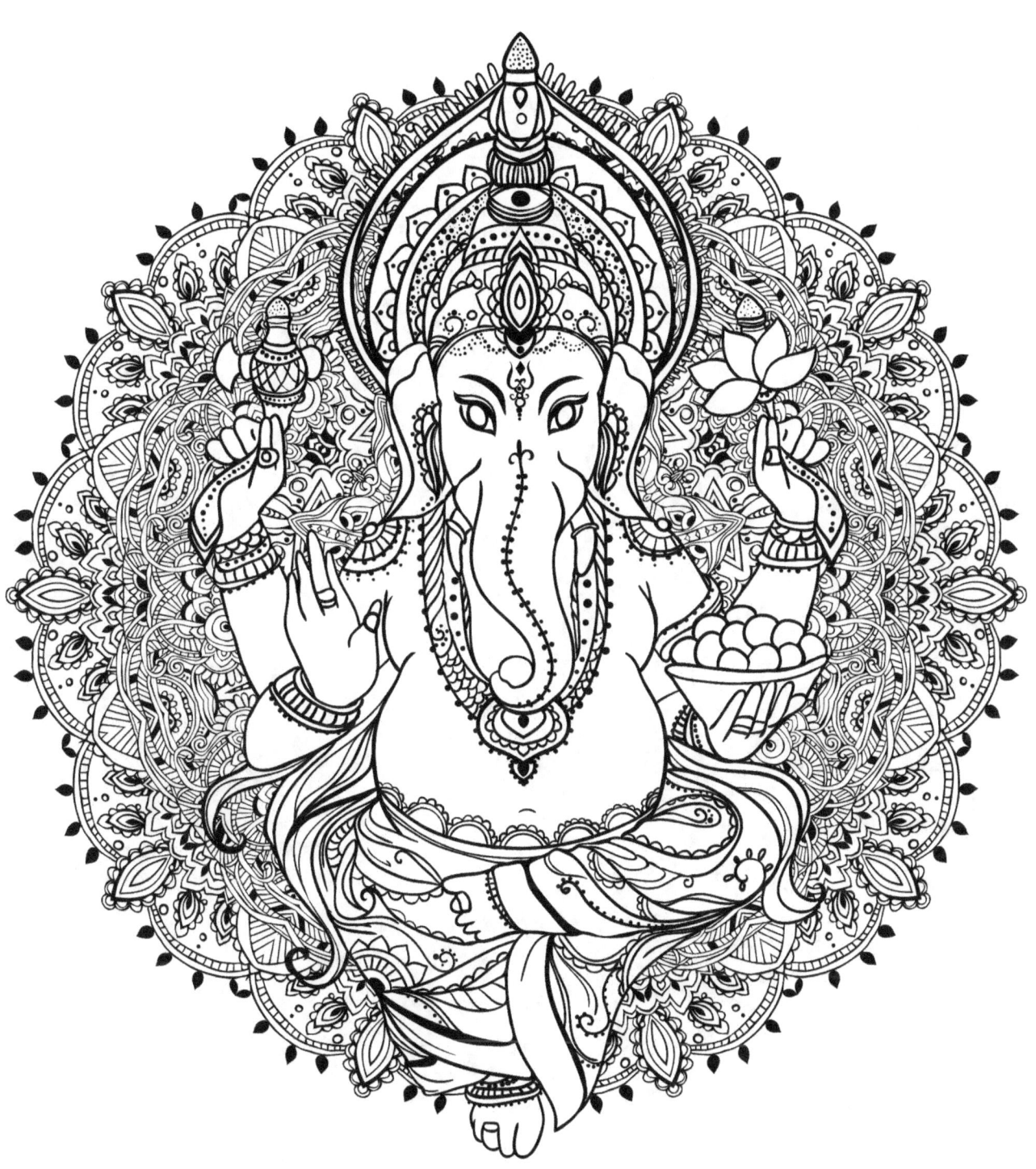

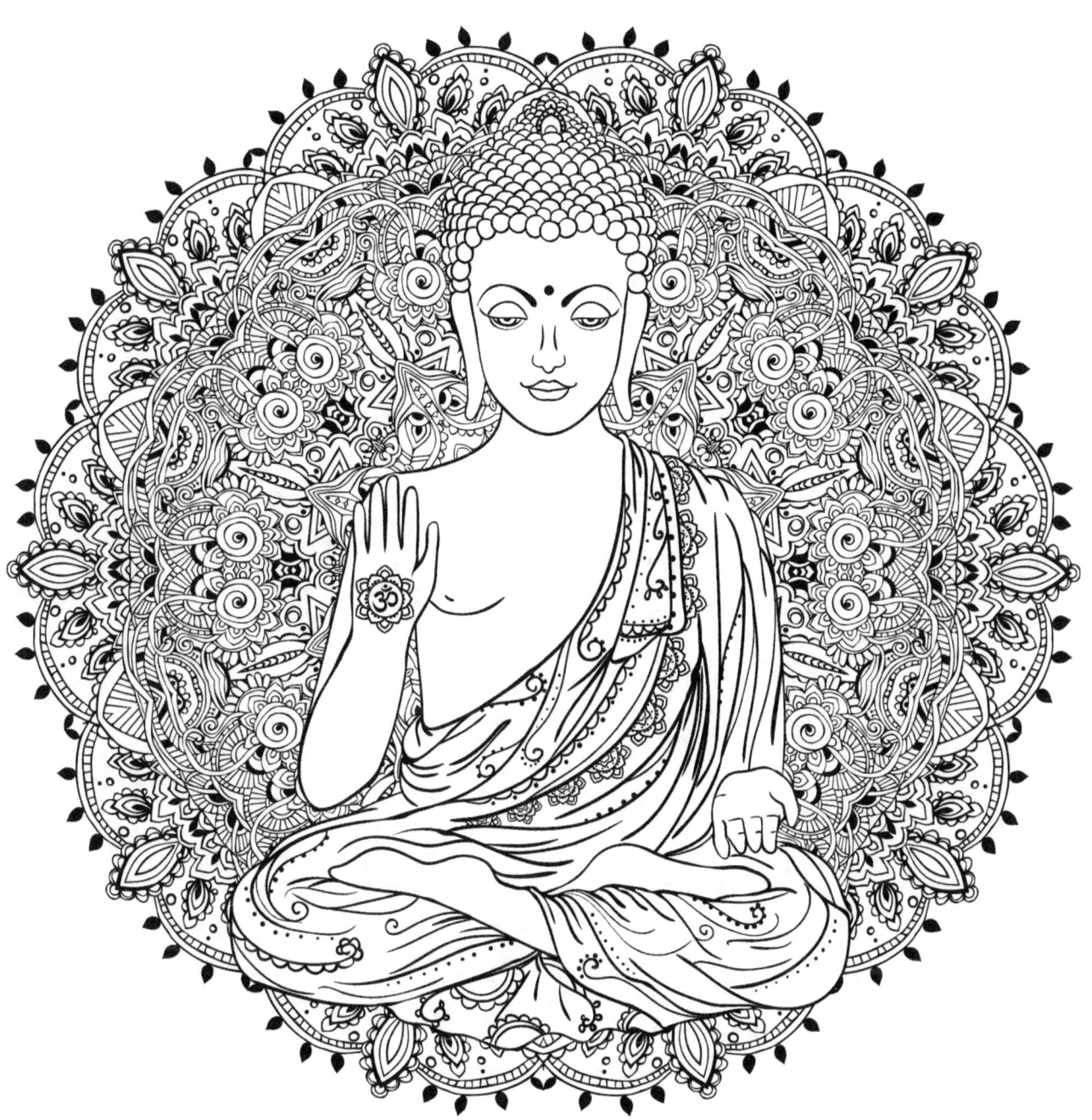

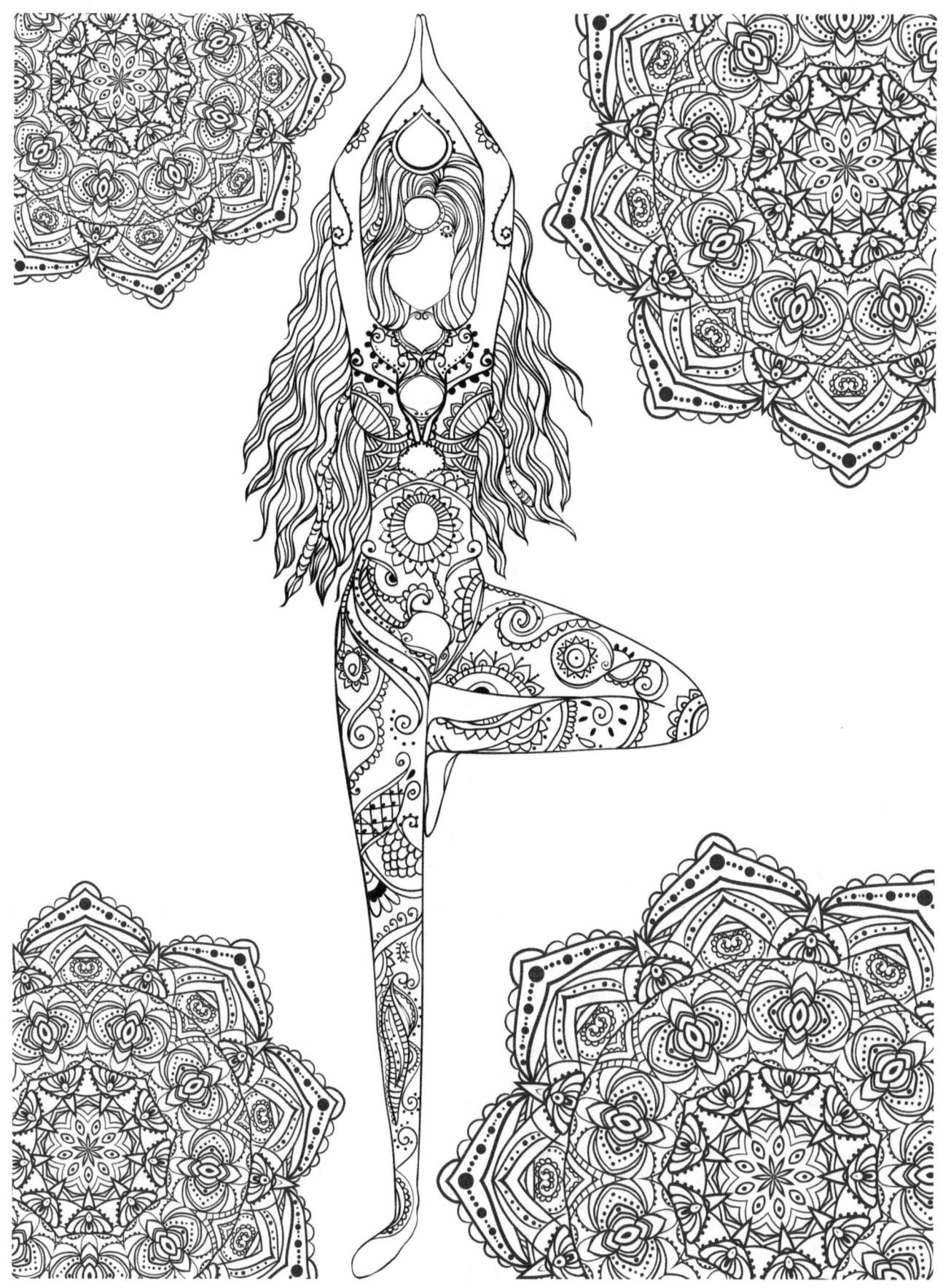

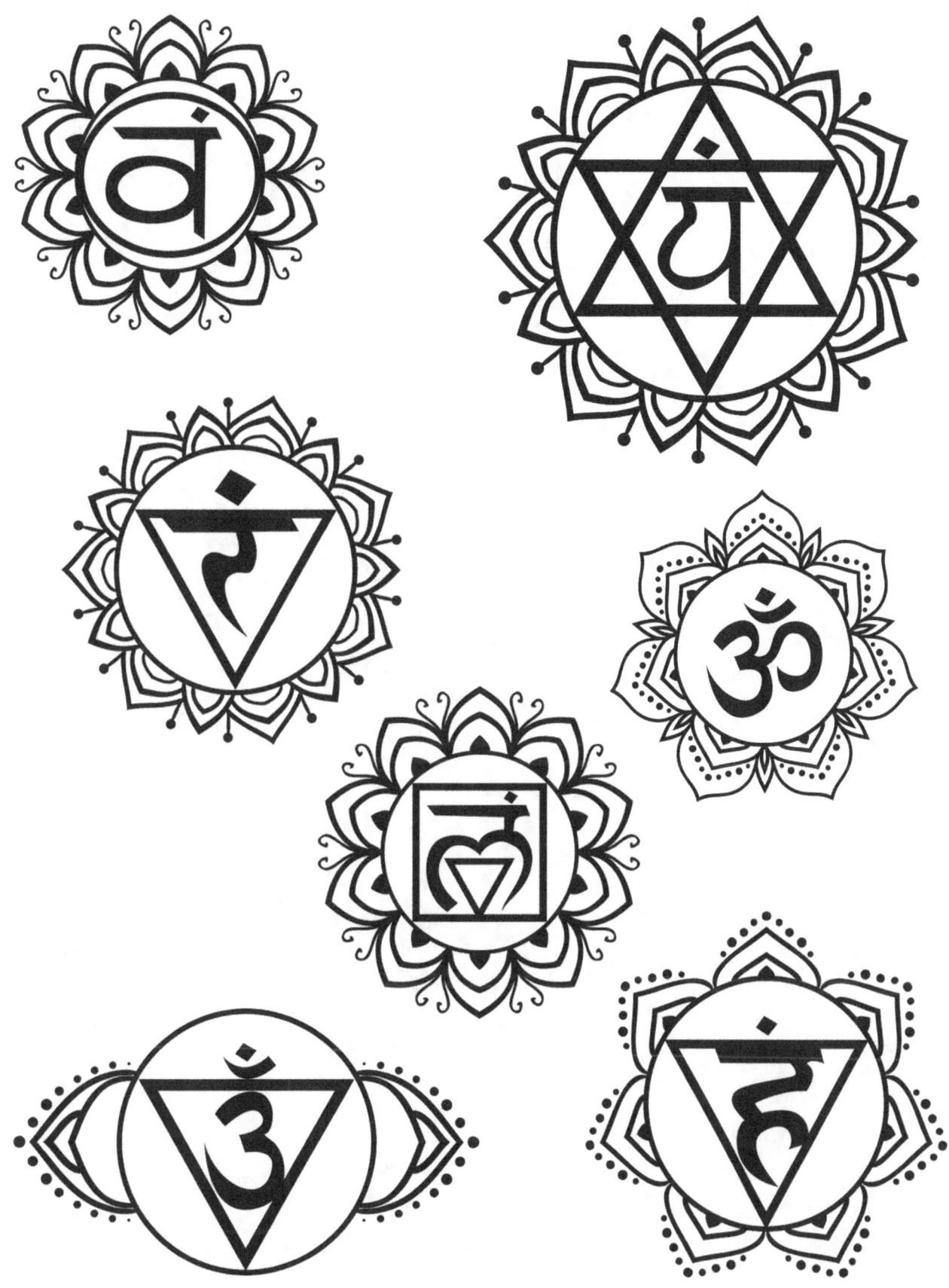

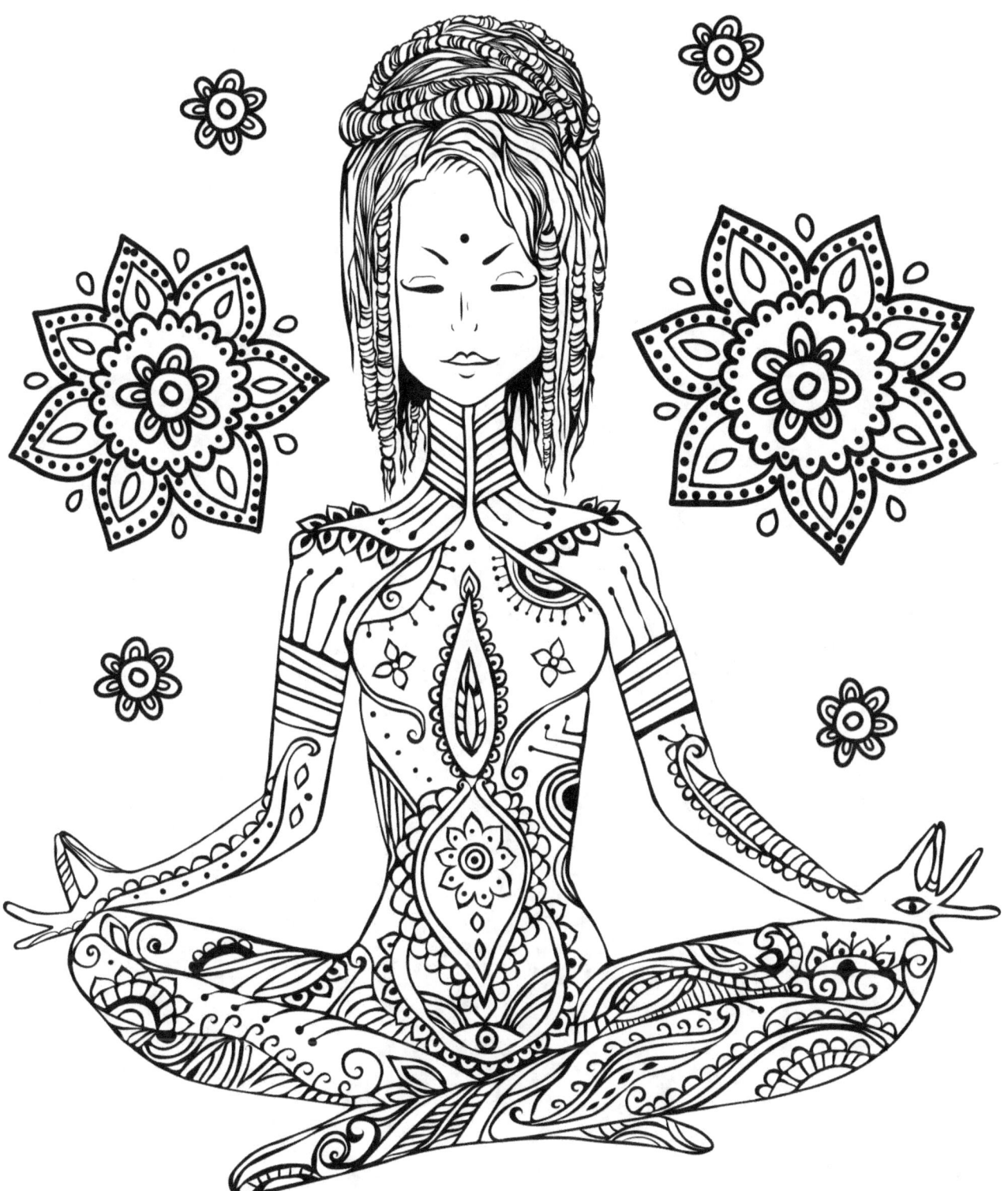

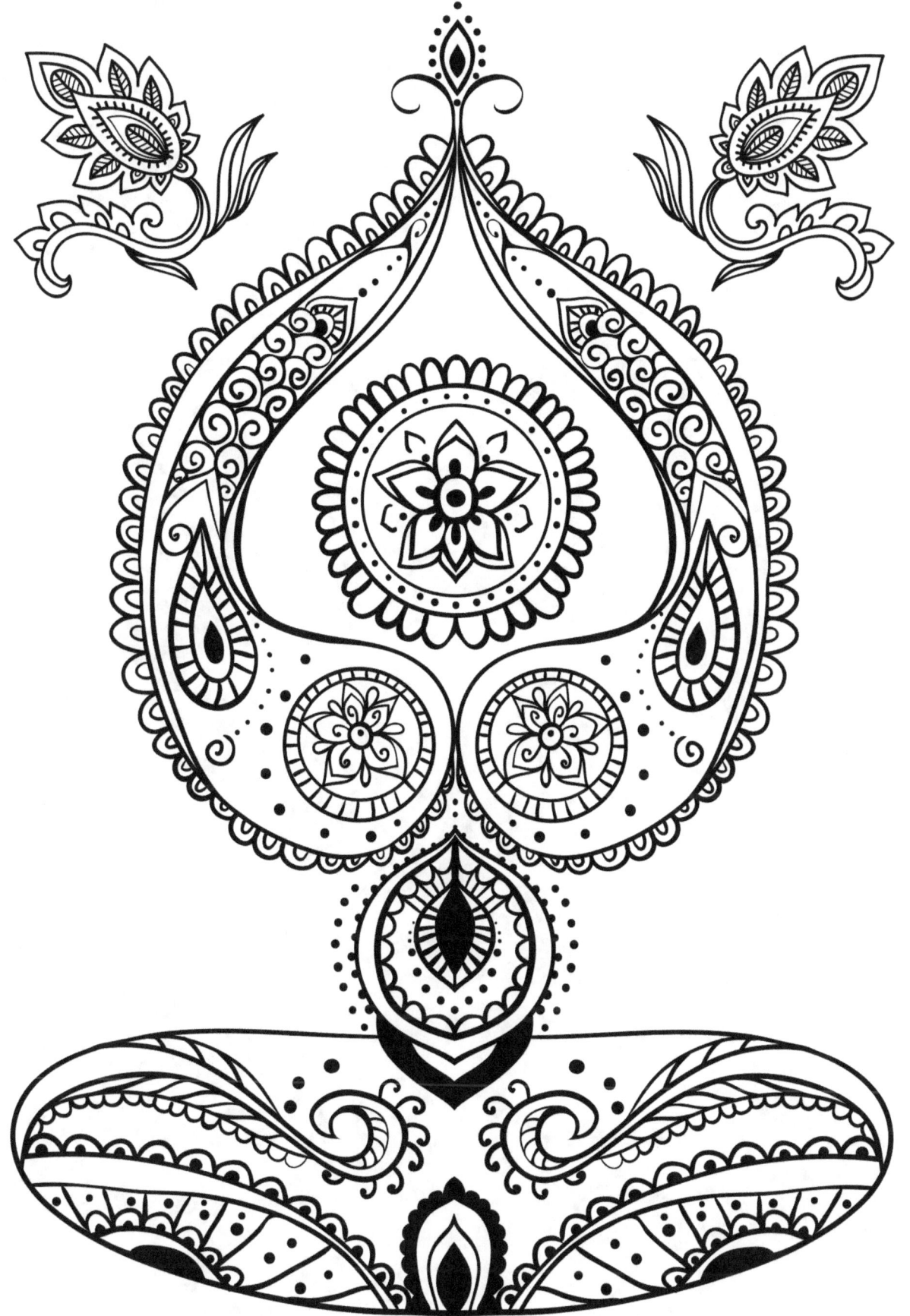

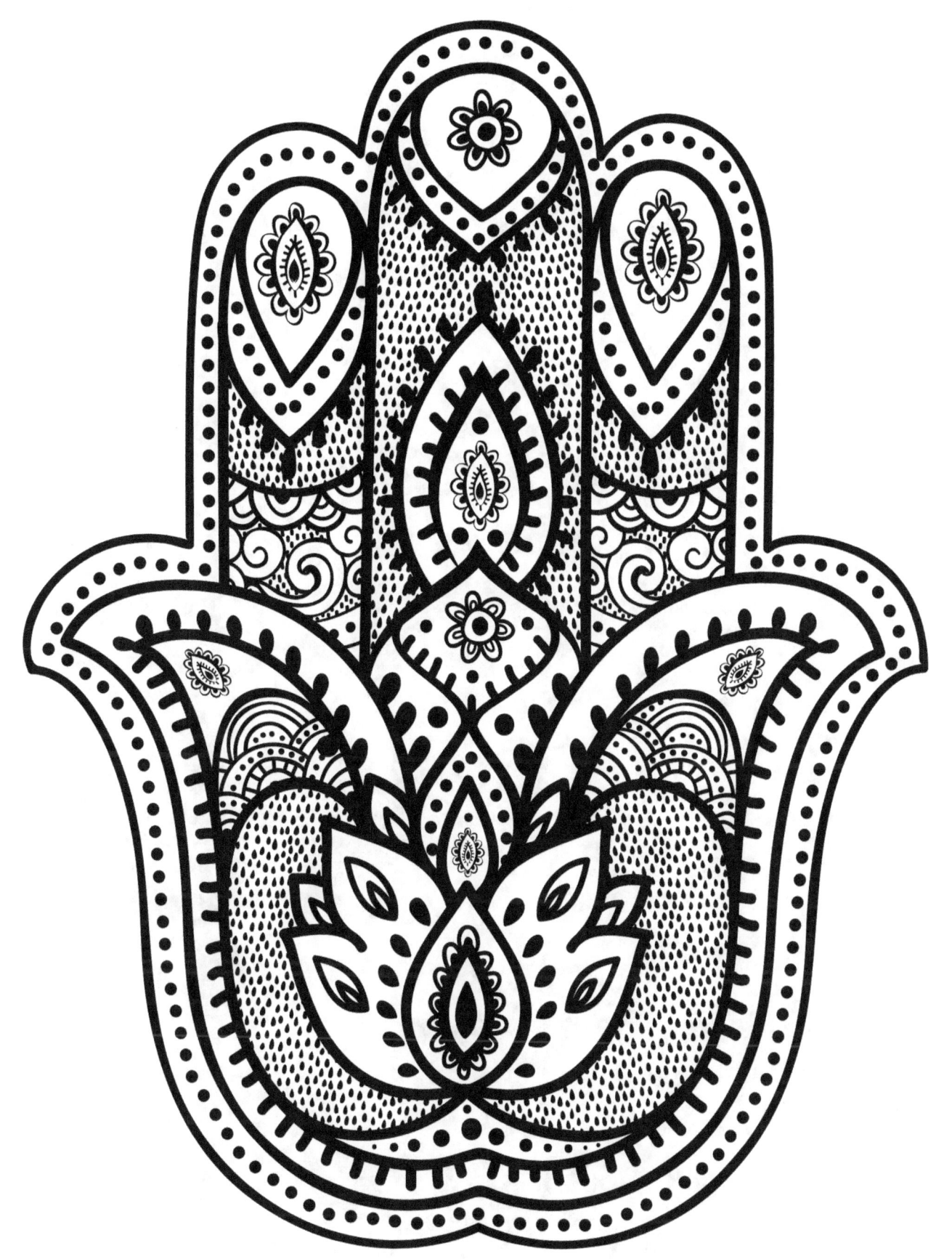

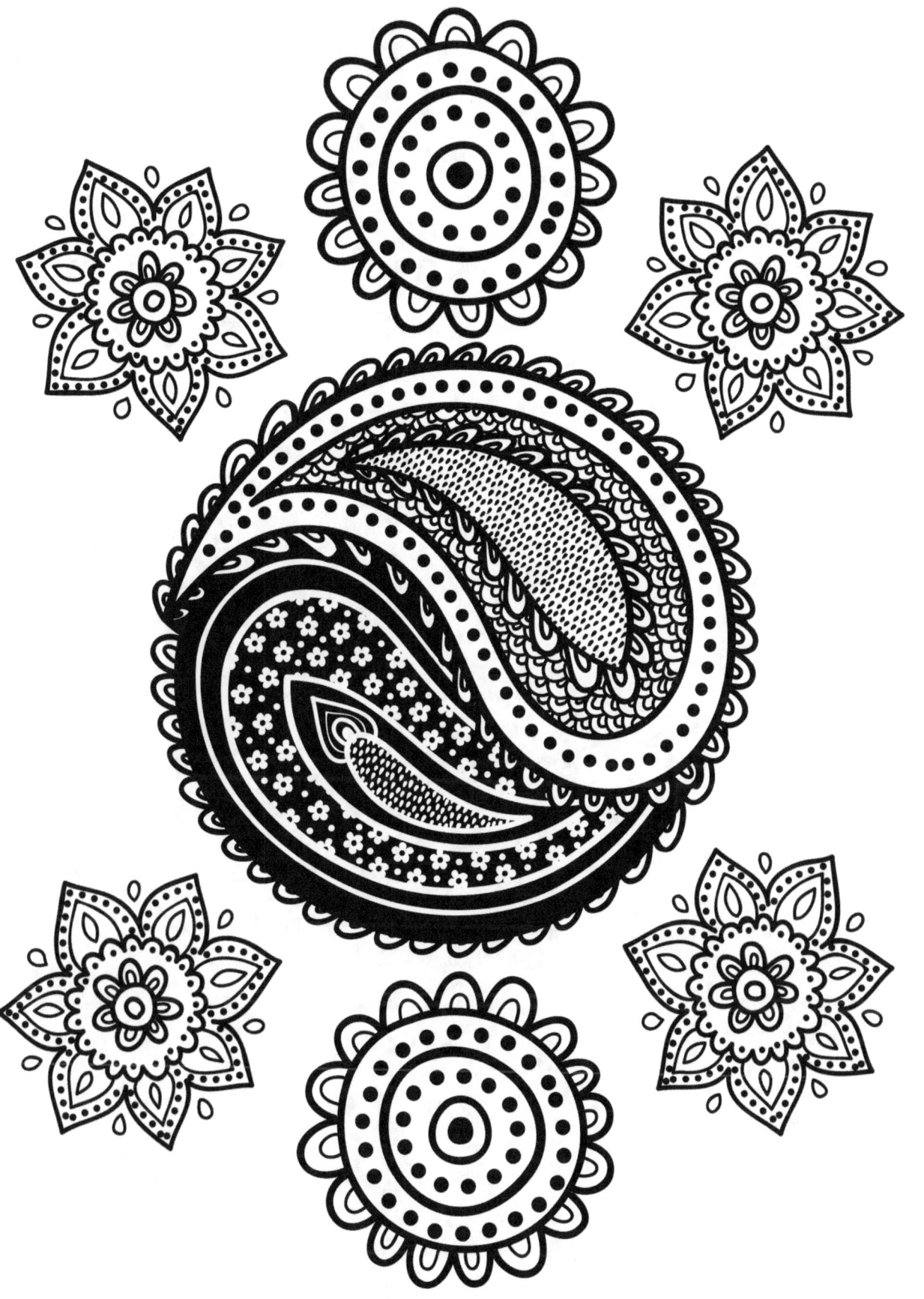

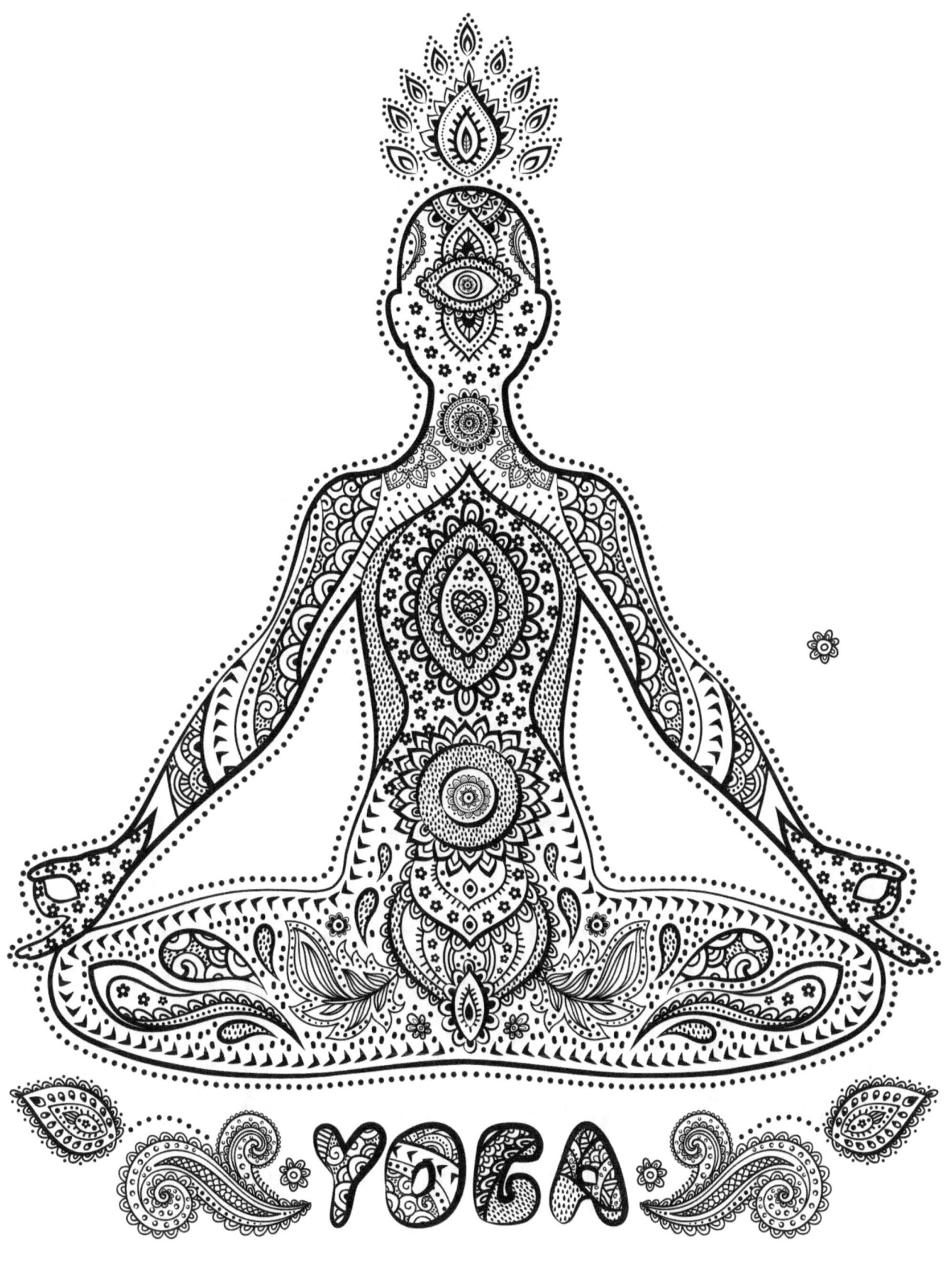

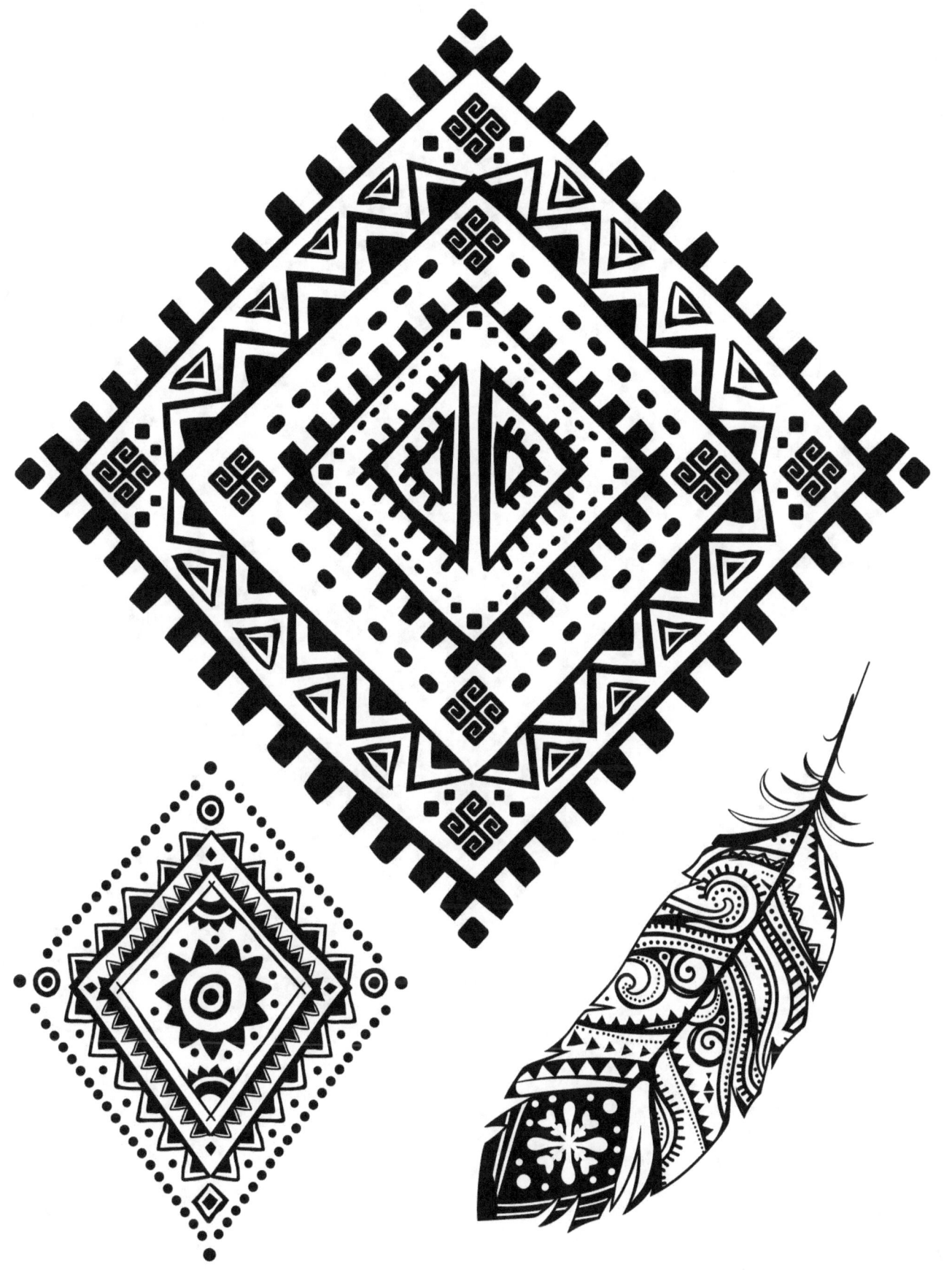

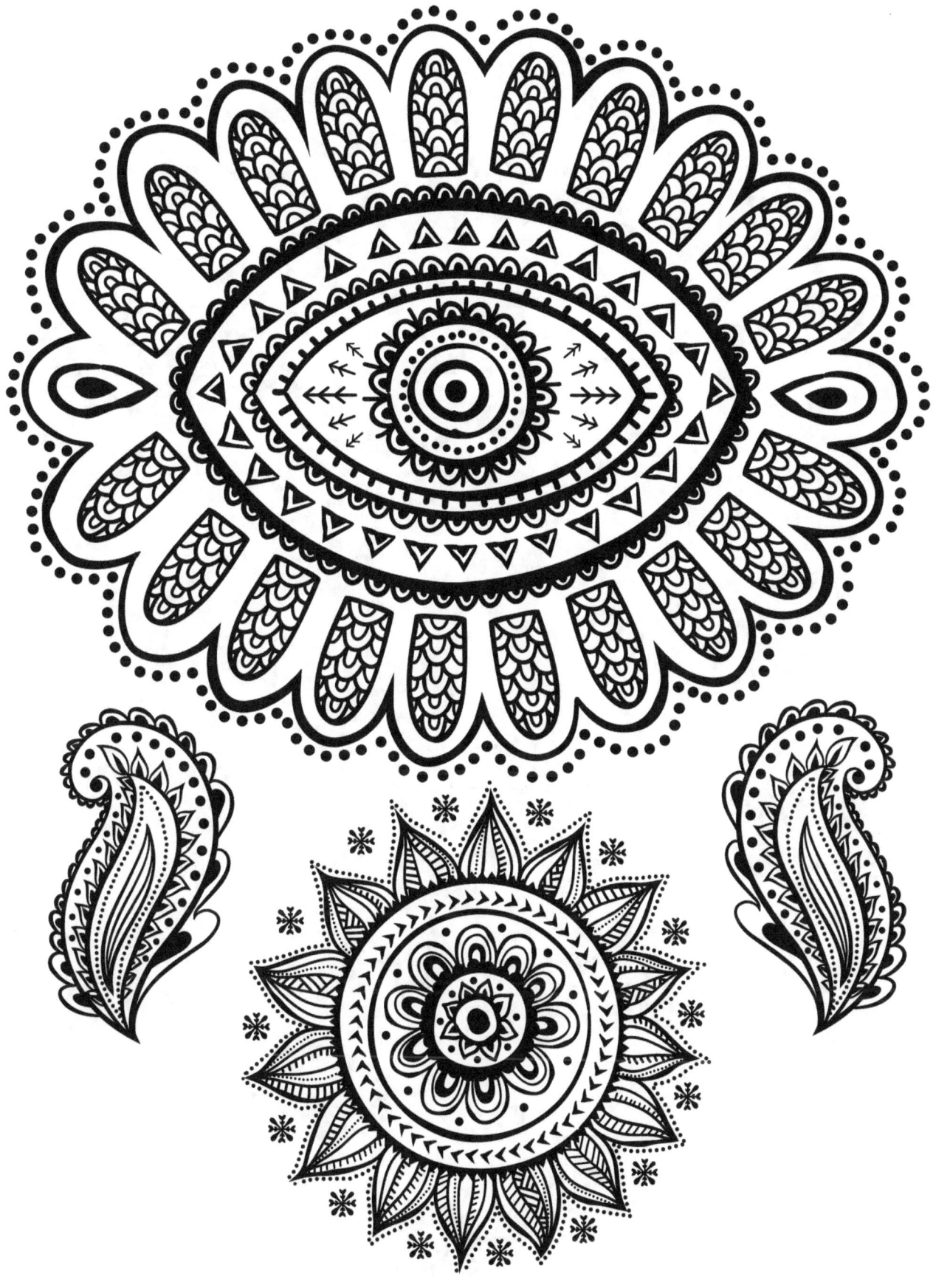

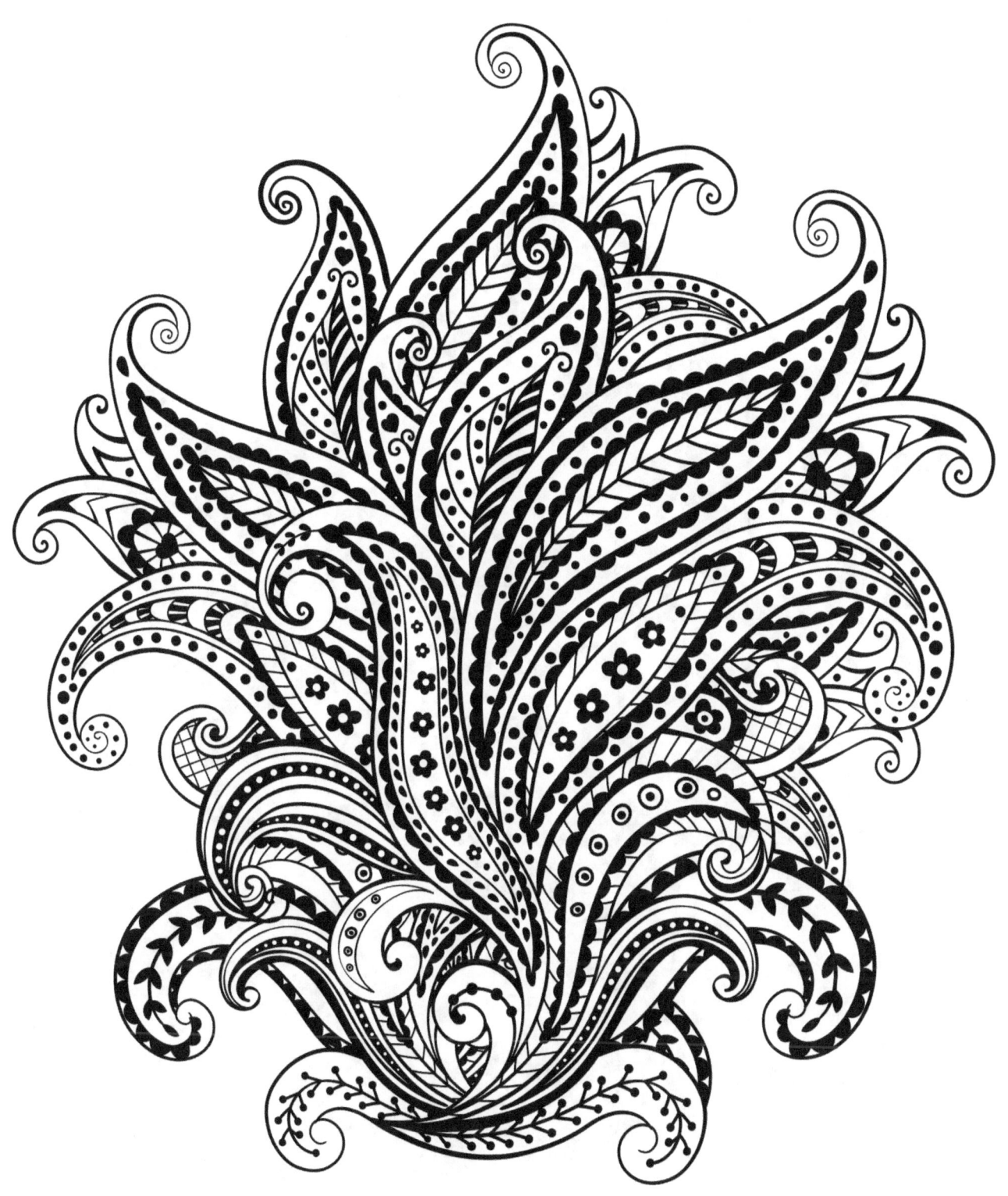

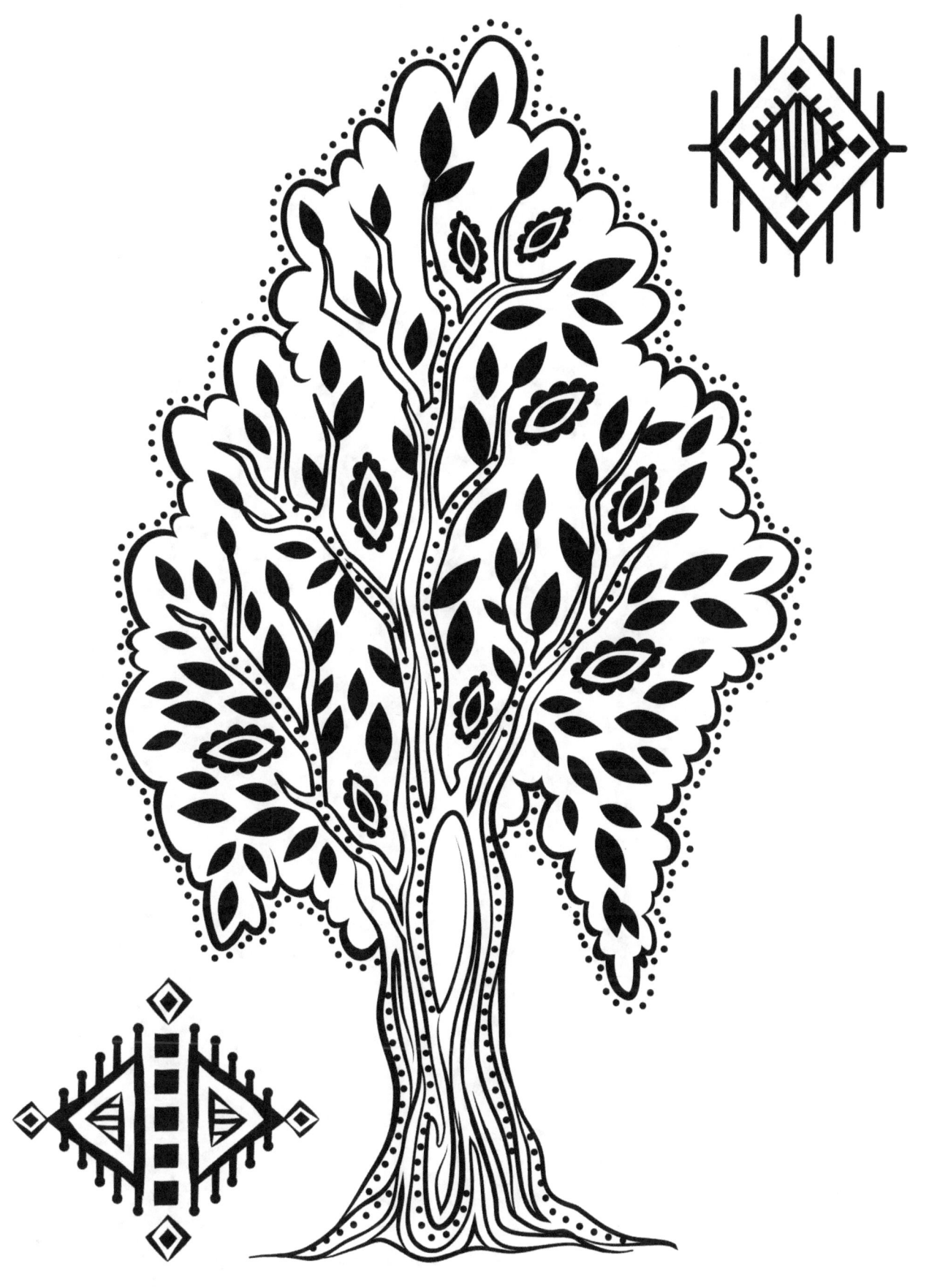

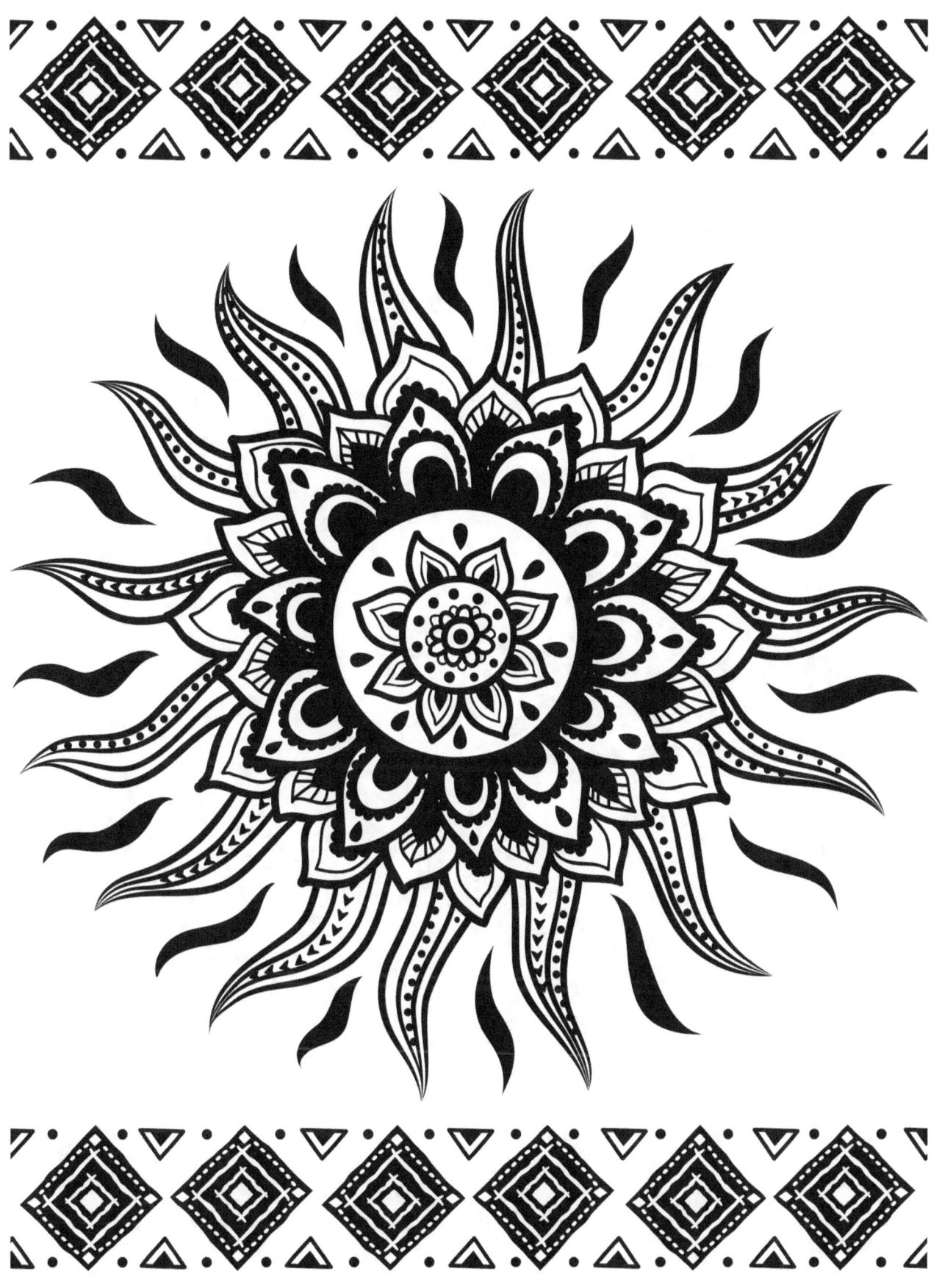

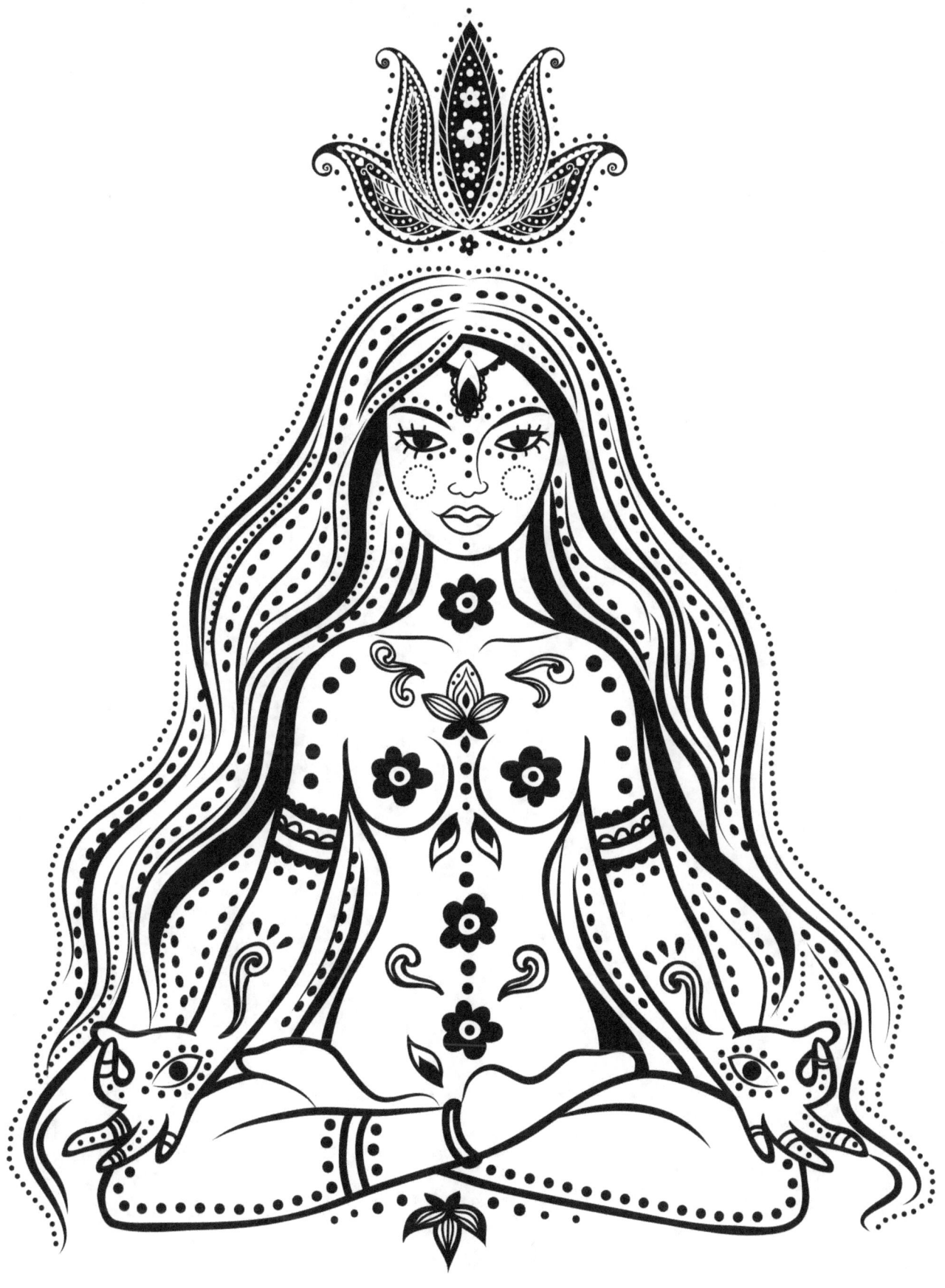

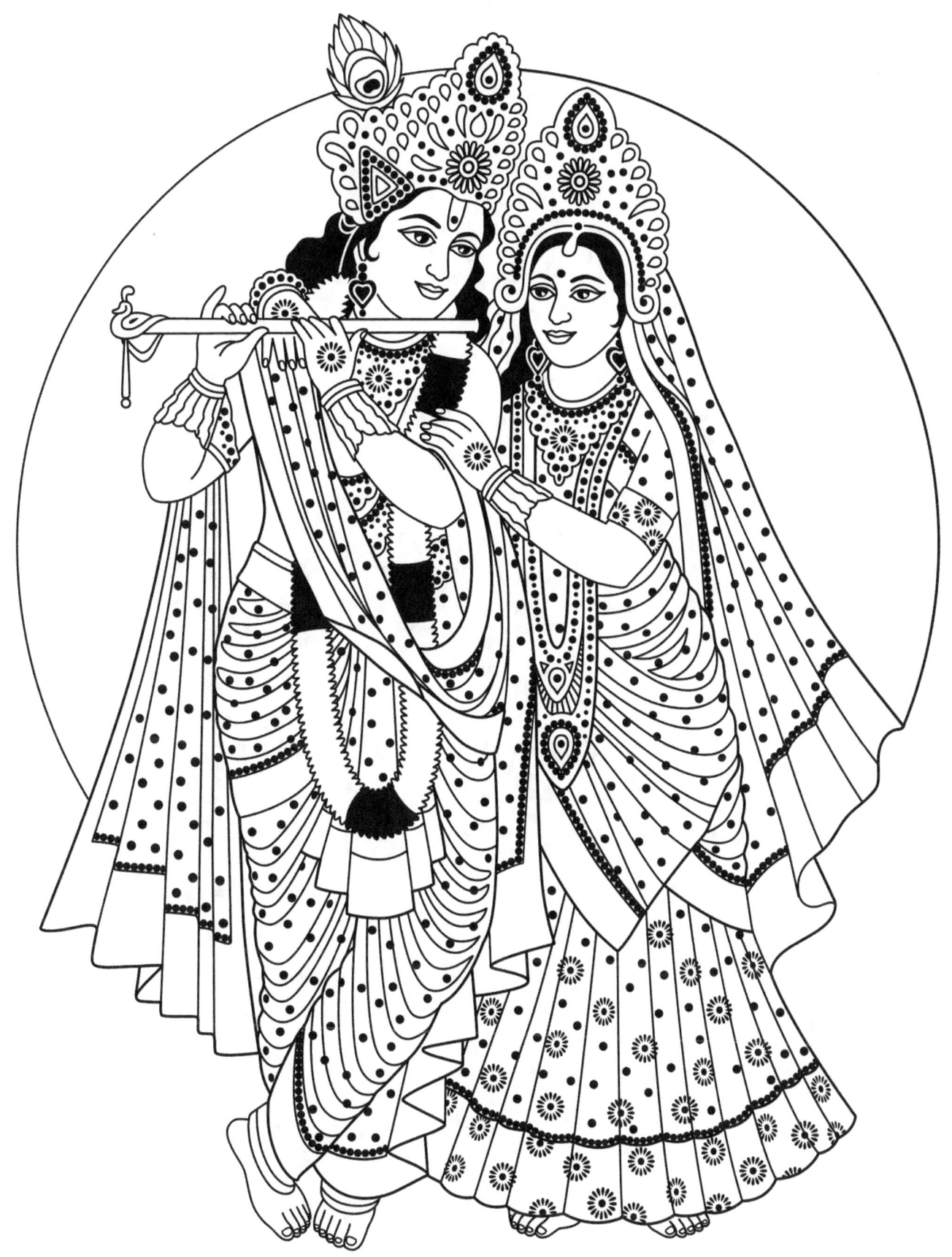

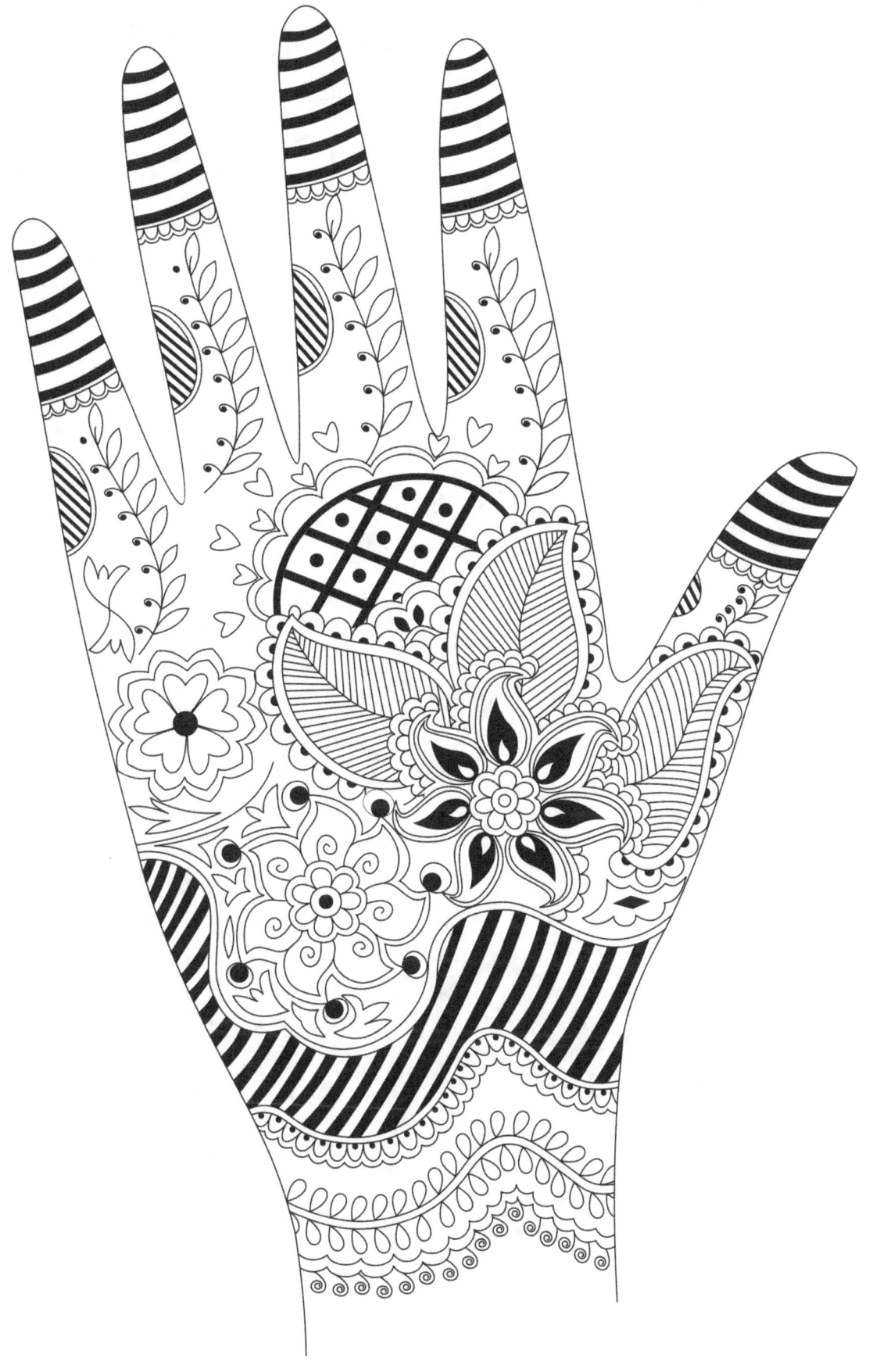

www.ingramcontent.com/pod-product-compliance
Lightning Source LLC
Chambersburg PA
CBHW081558170526
45166CB00009B/2733

* 9 7 8 1 5 1 9 6 9 4 0 5 8 *